THINK LIKE A STARTUP

Get Agile and Unleash Your Inner Entrepreneur

STEVE SAMMARTINO

WILEY

First published as *The Lessons School Forgot* in 2017 by John Wiley & Sons
Australia, Ltd

42 McDougall St, Milton Qld 4064

Office also in Melbourne

This edition first published in 2020 by John Wiley & Sons Australia, Ltd

Typeset in 12.5/14.5pt Arno Pro

© Start Up Squad Pty Ltd 2017

The moral rights of the author have been asserted

ISBN: 978-0-730-38196-9

A catalogue record for this
book is available from the
National Library of Australia

Cover design by Wiley

Printed in United States of America by Quad/Graphics.

VA0D23BD9-872F-4333-A66D-A916F4A0B4DD_110519

Disclaimer

The material in this publication is of the nature of general comment only, and
does not represent professional advice. It is not intended to provide specific
guidance for particular circumstances and it should not be relied on as the
basis for any decision to take action or not take action on any matter which
it covers. Readers should obtain professional advice where appropriate, before
making any such decision. To the maximum extent permitted by law, the author
and publisher disclaim all responsibility and liability to any person, arising
directly or indirectly from any person taking or not taking action based on the
information in this publication.

Contents

About the author

Steve wrote his first lines of computer code at age 10, and is one of Australia's most respected business minds. While the school system didn't really suit his learning style, he has an incredible ability to make sense of how emerging technology is changing the way we work, live and earn. He's a born entrepreneur, and had his first startup at age 10 — an organic egg farm. While holding down a daytime corporate gig, in his spare time he started and eventually sold a successful a clothing business. (He used to start work at 5 am, sell to customers at lunch time and do the administration at night.)

After graduating from university majoring in Economics, he worked in multiple Fortune 500 companies and held many senior positions culminating in directorships, before answering his true calling for independence from The System. Curious about why some people seemed to get richer, regardless of education and income, he delved deeply into the study of personal finance, *informally*. His experience means he intimately understands small and big business and how to play the game to get ahead and design your own future.

Steve has had multiple technology startups, including launching rentoid.com, one of the first 'sharing economy' startups, before Uber or Airbnb. Steve had a successful exit selling the startup to a public company. He now invests in emerging technologies and has multiple advisory board positions in a variety of disruptive technologies across the airline, automotive, real estate and co-working industries, and the internet of things, quantified self, mobile applications, and 3D printing technologies.

Extreme projects are something Steve loves doing to demonstrate what is possible. Crowdfunded via Twitter, he helped build a full-size driveable car made from 500 000 Lego pieces, complete with an engine made completely from Lego that runs on air. This project has over 9 million views on YouTube and was a global news story. He also put a toy space ship into earth orbit for under $2000 to prove how cheap powerful technology has become.

A media commentator on technology and the future, Steve is a regular on the ABC and provides expert assessment on the rapidly evolving technology sector. He has also been featured on the BBC, The Smithsonian Institute, The Discovery Channel, Mashable, Wired, and has even had documentaries made about his projects. Steve wants to share a life of hacking the system with you, so you can use emerging technology to your advantage, to live the life you deserve.

Get in touch with him at stevesammartino.com.

Preface

The first job I ever had was in a factory. I was pretty excited about it at the time. The job would leave a permanent imprint on my life. There was something about it I've never forgotten; it changed me in a way. Maybe it was to do with all those routines, procedures and outputs, or maybe it was the way people behaved inside this closed system. In hindsight it all seemed a little strange, unnatural, even a little inhuman, but I didn't really question it when I was starting out — I just took it as the way things were.

Factories are without doubt among the most interesting kinds of workplace humans have created. Most of us have at some point had the opportunity to at least visit one and see it in action from close up. Maybe you were sent to the factory of a company you worked with, so you could get an understanding of how things were done there. Maybe you've partaken in a bit of industrial tourism — aviation and chocolate factories are favourites. If you haven't had such an experience, let me recall my factory job for you.

Most people would arrive for their shift at the last moment. Clad in uniform with the company logo emblazoned on it, we streamed through the factory gate, which was set into an eight-foot-high chain-link fence — I'm still not sure if it was designed to keep outsiders out or insiders in. The plant was broken up into sections, clearly delineated by yellow lines so everyone knew where to go and how to get there. More experienced workers took on more advanced tasks on the factory floor.

Right on 8.50 am a loud electronic bell heralded the start of the shift. In the next 10 minutes we'd all file inside to our workstations. Once the head count had been taken we would be allocated our tasks for the day. The work week, month and year were planned by management, our work clearly set out for us in advance.

Some of the day-to-day procedures took me a while to get used to. I had to work independently in semi-isolation yet in a large, crowded room. We had to memorise certain tasks and calculations, which was important so each of us maximised our output and the whole system worked efficiently. Conversation was generally discouraged, as was helping others on the shift, which we were told would end up slowing down two people instead of one. When we got stuck or needed help with a task, the shift manager was to be informed. But we soon understood it was important not to make mistakes, because it slowed down everyone on the production line.

To remind us of the policies (there were quite a few to remember), the walls were festooned with notices covering 'how-to' instructions, work-based targets, efficiency measures and reminders of what was required for success. Also displayed were photographs of star workers who had been recognised for performing above expectation on particular measures. And in every room a clock hung front and centre so we could all keep abreast of the time and meet our deadlines, completing specified outputs before each break. While many of the tasks were boring and repetitive, we were reminded of the benefits of doing things well and in a timely fashion. In fact, everything seemed to be about time.

Management generally had a vantage point from which they could observe and assess the workers' progress. They'd walk the floor looking over our shoulders to ensure everything was humming along efficiently and we would meet the production targets set for the day.

I was told little about what was going on outside my section of the factory, but was encouraged simply to focus on the job in front of me and doing it well. So long as I displayed a basic amount of competence, I could expect to be promoted to a higher position, like most of those who came before me, a position where the work was more demanding yet also more rewarding. No one got promoted if their performance review wasn't up to scratch, so it was vital that I master and memorise by rote the more rudimentary procedures. Quarterly interim performance audits, and an annual review at year's end, determined our rate of advancement both at the plant and, eventually, to something bigger and better beyond it. The performance reviews noted the areas of improvement required by each individual. Doing well in one area and neglecting another wasn't good enough; management demanded that workers both followed procedures effectively and were well rounded.

Obedience mattered too. Suggesting a better way to do something, or questioning why we did certain things, was totally frowned on. I found it annoying that sometimes the most rewarded workers weren't the best, but rather the best behaved. Sometimes it felt like following rules and wearing the right uniform were considered more important than the work itself, and the managers always had their favourites.

To be honest, I didn't like this job very much, but while I sensed the lack of freedom and humanity from day one, I somehow stuck it out for the next 13 years. If you're wondering why, it's because I didn't have much choice. I started this job when I was five years old, and my employer was the public schooling system.

While all the tasks and expectations were made exceptionally clear at this factory, there was one important thing I didn't realise until much later — the product I was making was myself. I was a raw material being processed into something that could be sold in the marketplace. The factory of school was teaching me to be a successful participant in the industrial economy. I was being prepared to be marketed to the industrialists who owned and controlled the factors of production. They would eventually take on a form of quasi-ownership of this 'human resource', otherwise known as Steve Sammartino. Perhaps they owned you too — maybe they still do?

Together in this book, we'll be undertaking a journey towards independence. Because I believe something was stolen from many of us through subterfuge. In the course of the book we'll explore this system that shaped you, and I'll help you unlearn its mode of thinking and relearn the lost art of self-reliance. Along the way I'll introduce you to some cool tools, new rules and general life hacks that will enable you to design your own system for living. One designed by you, for you. And you're going to love it.

Part I
Revolution

There's a lot of material in the market these days on the technology revolution. Disruptive technology is very much the management focus du jour. The impact it has on the economy, industry and established industrialised companies has been well documented. And it makes sense to seek insights into how companies facing it might be able to respond. What's less clear is how the heck an individual with a skill set that is about to expire might cope with the impending changes. If companies, industries and economies are worried about what might come next, and their potential displacement, then the people who make up these organisations have reason for their own concerns. I hope that this book will become a timeless future-proofing manifesto for your own economic survival. The techniques and ideas in here mash up economic ideas that have survived millennia with a new set of technological tools with which to implement them. To make this work, I've split the book into three discrete sections that give context, structure and strategy under the headings Revolution, Revenue and Reinvention.

Part I, 'Revolution', outlines how we got here, why most of us believe what we do and act the way we do, and why as a result so many of us struggle financially and in our careers. This background helps makes sense of how we have been shaped to think in certain ways, even when this runs counter to our own interests. It describes the obsolete mindset we need to escape from and sets out a new philosophy to help us reframe our thinking and to reinvent ourselves. It points towards the *aha* moment when we can finally say, screw the system, I can change — and now I know what's possible. I believe the links between the traditional institutions of the school and industrial economic model are really important and can't be overstated. Understanding why systems and thinking developed in the way they did very often reveals the fork in the road we need. It's cathartic, lifting a weight off our shoulders and encouraging us to take a new direction without confusion or fear. It's an essential precondition for cutting new ground.

The revolution we are living through is redesigning how money moves around and what is valued in our world. You'll learn about the exponential growth of the technologies behind the changes, but also that, surprisingly, the power skills of the emerging era are not purely technological, but human and creative too; they are skills anyone can learn if they make the effort. This revolution is for everyone who chooses to participate. I hope you'll be inspired to *unlearn* some of the upside-down thinking you were taught at school and *relearn* that you were born an entrepreneur brimming with creativity. The first chapters will expose the myth that we are all headed for economic hardship. Some surely are, but it is really a choice they make; you need not do so. Economic hardship today is a result of personal stagnation, because we have never known such opportunity, and it is at the same time so affordable (free is a pretty compelling price point). This revolution we've all been gifted to participate in is made possible by a level of prosperity unmatched in human history, a time of great abundance for those who recognise the shift and decide to take advantage of it. You'll soon know that this revolution was actually designed with you in mind, but it requires you to be active and shape it for yourself.

CHAPTER 1
A lesson about school

It's time to launch the Startup of you!

We are in the midst of a technological revolution. There is no doubt that our world is changing at a pace never before witnessed in human history. This is no longer controversial, or even debatable; it's a mere fact. We've seen it in our own lives. Innovations that would have seemed unimaginable even 10 years ago are now widely available, affordable and so much a part of our daily life that we imagine we couldn't live without them. But it's still early days. We're only 20 years into this, and let's not forget that the automobile didn't arrive until 150 years after the start of the industrial revolution.

This technological shift is impacting us all at a societal and economic level, changing the very nature of the lives we live, including of course how we earn a living. No one is immune. Incredible changes are being introduced in every industry, every business model, every job. This is because everyone is sharing the same core digital technologies.

This revolution is open to everyone who chooses to participate. But we need to reboot the entrepreneurial spirit every one of us was born with, because school, with all its good intentions, has not prepared us for this.

STEM is not enough

As the birth child of the industrial revolution, school taught us survival skills for a bygone era. Educators and governments have deftly moved to ensure the graduates of tomorrow arrive prepared for the technological era by focusing on what they call STEM subjects — *Science, Technology, Engineering* and *Maths*. The problem is that STEM is not enough. In fact, this re-emphasis, on its own, really won't help much at all, because it is just more of what we've been taught historically, with a different angle of approach. What we need to do is add the two missing E's of *Economics* and *Entrepreneurship*, so STEM becomes ESTEEM.

By adding the missing E's, we have a chance to build people's esteem. We give people an opportunity to become more human and to live an adventure as modern-day economic explorers carving out a new path for themselves. When we share the lost arts of entrepreneurship and self-reliance, a spark we all had as kids is reignited so brightly that it becomes a beacon to guide others.

ESTEEM recognises that we need each other, that some non-technical skills, as you'll see, create value that makes previously invisible STEM visible. They create more value than is offered by anything else we attempt, because without the spirit of exploration, even in an economic sense, we'd all still be living in caves. Building an economy around the idea of ESTEEM means appreciating the wide variety of viewpoints and natural faculties we have to offer. Tech Hackers, Design Hipsters and Sales Hustlers meet in the middle and make something great together. When we add the missing E's we give everyone who believes they have a chance a tilt at an independent future. If we want future-proof kids, and grown-ups, we all need ESTEEM.

For too long science and maths have been largely ignored in wider society. We glorify celebrity and sporting achievement, but technologists are rarely recognised. I've lost count of how many sports people have been named Australian of the Year; it really is 'fall of Rome' stuff. But it does feel like the tide is turning. As end users of technology, society is starting to value science on a personal level, and it's about time. More and more kids are learning to code, to hack, to experiment with robotics — it feels like an exciting shift. But if we reconfigure their minds only to science, without addressing economics and entrepreneurship, we are still just teaching them to participate in someone else's game, and we all deserve more than that.

We need to be able to take what we know and convert it into income, to participate in the market not only to get a good job but also to *create* jobs for ourselves and others. Even better, we can look towards inventing new industries that don't even exist yet, and all the technology in the world can't do that, because technology without practical application, in the form of customers and a market, is just a discovery. The people developing the wizardry of tomorrow deserve to be the beneficiaries of what they create. In fact, anyone doing anything deserves the dignity of knowing how to manage their own future, and this is what *Think Like a Startup* is all about.

Time to unlearn

For the sake of collective progress, let's assume we're all late to the party. We probably should have started a little earlier on all this. Yes, there's always someone who knows more and started before us — so what? Let's agree that the second best time to start is now. And the first thing we have to do before anything else is unlearn the way we think. In order to reinvent ourselves, we need to wipe our human hard drive clean of all the useless files we've been carrying around since school. Some of them are heavy and slowing us down. We need to remember that our training to follow a linear path is obsolete. With some simple knowledge hacks, we can reframe what looks risky and pursue a new path.

Today's playbook can be learned relatively quickly, once we free our mind from what we have been told. It's low cost and has a high return on time invested. The least anyone willing to have a crack at reinventing themselves can expect is that they'll get a very nice ROH (return on humanity). Sometimes the having is in the doing, and by doing more than you've done in the past, you'll become more than you were and will feel pride at having had the guts to try. And some strange things happen when we invest in ourselves. We gain a great deal of self-esteem, and our own economics improves because we know, and others sense, we are the kind of person to make an effort. It's the same feeling you get when you've prepared well for anything: suddenly the outcome doesn't seem as important, although we are often happy with it.

You've already got the skills you need. If you can read, you can do it. I really mean that. This revolution is one that connects skills and people, and we all need each other. But if you can dig up some deeply buried desire for risk, some courage and a bit of the creative spirit you had as a five-year-old, then I know you'll seize the opportunity that being connected to everyone in the world can bring. It's an opportunity no generation before ours ever had.

The history of the present

Before we can unlearn anything, we need to know why we sometimes think the way we do. We need to be able to see through the system that shaped us. School is a good place to start.

The first thing you need to know about school is this:

SCHOOL WAS NOT DESIGNED WITH YOU IN MIND.

They designed it for them. You might be wondering who 'they' actually are. Well, 'they', in the developed world at least, are the governments and the industrialists and business leaders who own and control the factors of production. School as we know it was designed to create competent, compliant workers who could fit into the rapidly industrialising world.

Before the industrial revolution there was a very high probability that people would simply do what their parents did, especially if it involved agriculture or a craft. They would follow family tradition, the required skills usually handed down from parents or close relatives. Or they'd work in the family business, most often eking out a living with the primary focus of providing for the food, clothing and lodging to sustain their family. There wasn't much excess for the working classes, but there was a fair amount of freedom.

Why change hurts

If you're wondering why change is so hard for us to cope with, it's because we've been programmed for stability, indoctrinated from the age of innocence to believe in a system that is now obsolete. From the moment we are capable of comprehension, we are shaped into little industrialised robots awaiting instructions from the corporate or governmental algorithm. It's not our fault that change is so uncomfortable. The 200 years of the industrial era, despite its world wars and depressions, led to a long period of systemic stability and unsurpassed material prosperity. For many generations we have had the formula for living an increasingly prosperous life, and the industrial revolution delivered against this promise big time.

As I wrote in my first book, *The Great Fragmentation*, we now live better than royalty did before this revolution, and anything that threatens to upend that comfort is fearsome. We fret at the possibility of change not only because we've never had it so good, but because we've been told all our lives to leave the big important stuff to the people in charge of the systems in which we obediently participate. Economically we have been coddled, so much so that we have come to believe our system was designed to serve us in perpetuity. It's now clear that is not going to be the case. The system is changing dramatically, and we need to change our personal business models to recognise this. We have a choice:

We can wait for the system to get better.

Or we can reinvent ourselves, redesigning our lives and in the process helping reshape the system (which I go into in detail in Part III, 'Reinvention').

We've been treated like economic outpatients waiting for the government and our once reliable institutions to provide for us, believing they will provide us with the opportunities we need, and all our social and economic needs, so long as we work hard. It's not surprising we think like this — they trained us to think they would continue to provide jobs and security. Well, they're not going to. The incentive structure of management tells the simple tale of why it can't and won't happen.

Incentives shape behaviour

Nothing indicates what people will do more clearly than their incentives. These days our economic lives, which can be loosely equated to 'the market', are an aggregation of short-term interests. Government and corporate leaders simply aren't around long enough to care about the impact of the major decisions they make. In Australia, where I live, the federal government has three short years in which to allocate the resources at their disposal to improve the country for their constituents; in the USA it is four years, ending with a full year of campaigning. The average reign of a Fortune 500 CEO is 4.9 years[1], yet the average annual pay for the said CEO is now US$13.8 million, which is 204 times the median wage of the workers they lead.[2]

Leaders are incentivised to make decisions that maintain their position. Even if they have shares in the company, which is meant to align their interests, invariably they'll focus on making the balance sheet sing while they're in charge. So they'll avoid long-term, financially painful shifts in favour of short-term maintenance. If it makes it worse for the company later on, they won't care, because they'll be sitting under a palm tree somewhere with their multimillion-dollar severance 'go away' money. Wouldn't that be nice! Some other overpaid CEO will happily have a crack at cleaning up the mess.

And, you guessed it, the average politician makes the same play. They throw good money after bad in declining industries to keep people in jobs and their approval ratings high. In Australia we've experienced the same industrial upheavals most developed nations have gone through as low-cost foreign labour markets have improved their penetration of the manufacturing sector. In 2017 the auto industry as we know it finally shut down in Australia. It was of course inevitable. Australia, with its high wages, relatively small population and geographical remoteness from its main trading partners, could not continue to compete in a rapidly globalising market where trade barriers and tariffs are being reduced. But here's what our local government did: they subsidised the industry. When the gig was clearly up, they paid wealthy global corporations to keep the pretence of manufacturing in Australia.

Up until 2013 the auto industry in Australia received an annual $550 million in subsidies.[3] Car maker Holden, a wholly owned subsidiary of General Motors, has a market capitalisation of $50.5 billion, but received from our government an equivalent of $50 000 per employee per year in subsidies.[4] In the long run, the money invested on behalf of taxpayers becomes a sunk cost that could have gone into retraining and facilitating the development of future-proof industries more suited to the Australian (insert your country here) economic setting.

Hack the system!

I believe our education system won't and actually can't change fast enough. Given this, and the fact that probably everyone reading this has already completed their formal schooling, I wanted to write a book that brings together a way to hack the system. Something that pulls together some of the important lessons we have to teach ourselves, lessons that may have more social and economic value than our formal education gave us. This is not a book about what modern education could or should look like; it is about how to get what you want in life *despite* the system's failings. It gives you a bunch of tools to take your future into your own hands, things that blew my mind when I discovered them and wondered why they had never appeared on the blackboard. I want to start you on a process of re-education so you can grasp the fundamentals of life, the economic system and how to manage them to shape your life in whatever way you choose. By the end of the book you should be able to better understand the system you live inside, the way this system has shaped you and how to unlearn its bad bits. You'll understand some fundamentals about money, and how to future-proof yourself and any company in which you have an influence. Embrace what this book has to offer and you'll put yourself in a great position to leverage the technological era we are entering.

The little history lessons in this chapter are important because they help us understand why so many questions about economic and life issues go unanswered when we venture out into the world. Grasping the basic design principles of the school, it becomes clear why there are so many lessons that school seems to have forgotten — lessons that are vital to a happy life, lessons we have to teach ourselves and those we care about most. I want to provide short cuts and offer a template with which we can teach ourselves and, importantly, to suggest a survival philosophy.

When we discover the methods that once led to success have become obsolete, it's time to question everything we know in life about economics and technological reality. So strap yourself in for the ride. The industrial age is over; it's time we reinvented our future in a way that suits us, not them. We sure as hell can't rely on 'them', those who got us into this mess in the first place, yet they did pass on some pretty radical tools for those of us with a positive mindset. And the good news is we can choose to change our minds on what is possible for us.

CHAPTER 2
A proxy for happiness

The industrial economy introduced a range of linear incentives and expectations that made complete sense when they were developed. It went something like this:

Go to school & Study hard & Get qualified & Get a good job with a stable company & Have a happy life.

You'll have heard this before. It was the narrative passed onto me by my parents. They did so for very good reason: it was literally the formula for financial success during the 20th century. But it requires some reading between the lines to understand its meaning, and once we do this we can see that the script for the in-between bits has changed without notice. Particularly the last two elements:

» *Get a good job with a stable company:* This was a cognitive short cut for the idea that you'd have a better chance of earning more money, for a longer period of time, with greater advancement possibilities and in better working conditions, under the financial umbrella of a big corporation. It was better than smaller companies because it had more power in the market and paid more than small businesses did. It also had the respect of the market, with a personal branding benefit for those who worked inside it. You could build a career in and around your big-company experience, earn above-average wages and do better than your parents did. Oh, and don't forget, you won't be picked by that good reputable firm unless you have the necessary formal qualifications. Qualifications spelt capability.

» *Have a happy life:* A good job earned good money, and money was the path to 20th-century happiness. The context of this one runs deep. We need to remember the world our parents and their parents emerged from. They didn't have access to the level of material comforts we do. And I'm not talking about toys and entertainment, but household articles we take for granted today like toiletries, overflowing cupboards, pantries and fridges, pushbutton heating and private transport on demand. This line of thinking has to be traced deeply, back to the lives of struggle and hardship endured by the generations that came before us. They lived through periods of war and economic depression when the most basic material necessities were in short supply for the working classes. So money became a proxy for happiness. Because if you had enough money, you could usually buy the things you needed, and with the things you needed how could you be anything but happy? So money was their yardstick for success in life. We've all since found that money doesn't come close to guaranteeing happiness, especially in a post-scarcity society. The times have changed, but many still believe this false proxy is valid.

The plan was for life to flow in a beautifully predictable, linear fashion:

Happiness comes from money — money comes from having a good job — a good job comes from a good (formal) education — a formal education comes from doing well at school — doing well at school requires following the rules.

Once we revisit the context of the cultural environment that shaped those who taught us, both at home and at school, we can understand why they encouraged us to think that way. Of course they had our best interests at heart. But if the formula was one that didn't suit your personality, your style, your way of thinking, then you'd be ostracised and your confidence might be shattered before you had even entered the post-school money game. Subconsciously society arranged us in a hierarchy: the more schooling you had, the higher up the ladder you'd be placed. Your potential and expectations would be a function of how far you rose in the pre-work system.

Sure, there were always exceptions, but for most of us our place in the hierarchy was ordained before we even started work. Forget the fact that our schooling was a limited test of our abilities and we might have incredibly valuable skills the system simply didn't recognise. None of that mattered; what counted was how we performed in the formal system. We had to conform to the schooling mindset and method in order to be chosen. The market might never find out how good we were and what we really had to offer, because we'd never be given the opportunity to show them what we could do outside of the exam template.

The education tightrope

By now there is a good chance you are thinking I am anti-school. Nothing could be further from the truth. Education is without doubt the cornerstone of all the possibilities I've taken advantage of in my life, and probably in yours too. It's just that school is far too destination focused. Once we reach secondary or high school, our options become more and more narrowly focused. By the time we reach grade 8 we start making 'career decisions' on which subjects we choose. Career decisions at a time when we still can't decide what we want to do on Friday night. If we stumble in a certain subject, we'll lose the opportunity to work through it. If we love a certain subject that happens to be less valued by the left-brain logic society, like art or drama, we'll be discouraged from pursuing it. If we fail in maths in grade 8, we won't be allowed to take it in grade 9, and if we don't have advanced maths how can we possibility go on to complete a reputable degree at university? If we change our mind on what path we want to follow in grade 11, we've missed out on the foundation years of subject X and we won't be allowed to change streams.

So we are forced to choose our science, arts or humanities path when we are relatively young, long before what is legally regarded as the age of reason. We are quickly siloed into our 'chosen' trajectory for the remainder of our secondary schooling. School shifts from general to specific learning very quickly indeed. We are no longer learning how to learn; rather, we are learning how to pass tests in certain subject areas. We memorise specific information, which entitles us to continue to focus on that subject at a higher level. The ultimate goal is to pass through the final gate to formal qualification.

Let's say you want to be an accountant or an engineer — traditional industrial-era vocations. From grade 9 you will have taken the particular subjects that prepare you for this career. If you don't undertake the prerequisite subjects in your final years in school, you can't study for this career at university. If you don't have the university degree, you won't be considered by potential employers. It's equally frustrating if you become qualified in an area that doesn't turn out to be what you hoped for — just ask any lawyer you know. Most soon learn it's less about using the law to create a more humane society and more about nailing down every six minutes of billable time.

Our subject choices also have the judgemental weight of society behind them. It doesn't take us long to work out where our teachers and colleagues place us in the intellectual hierarchy. The smartest kids with the most potential are those who happen to be good at maths and science, the most valued subjects in a left-brain, logic-driven society. A small step down the hierarchy are respected humanities such as finance, economics and literature, and of course the bottom of the hierarchy is reserved for the artsy types, widely regarded as the flunkies of society, who are lucky if they can eke out any kind of career using their talents. Kids are persuaded, falsely, that most artistic pathways have little economic value and are best left as something we do on the side, in a 'post-success' environment. Which is ironic given how companies like Apple and Nike have risen above commodity-centric competition on the back of the artistic design of their products. In any case, why should we stop valuing given talents and passions solely on the basis of their limited economic potential? An economic limitation, mind you, that is quickly being reversed.

In the foundational years of schooling we learn the basics of learning itself. We learn what our brains and bodies are capable of. With very deliberate practice we acquire the ability to read, write and grapple with basic maths. We mix things up with art and play and creativity. We make things and use our bodies as tools. We explore sport and physical activity as part of our broader learning experience. We learn to play and collaborate with others and understand the human impact of working together. By the end of primary school we've built a solid base, from which most of us could still do anything with our lives. We graduate with our sense of creativity largely intact, and with an added set of intellectual possibilities at our disposal — ready for the real game of secondary school. In secondary school the basic building blocks of learning are used to start building a life. And this is where the educational pyramid scheme really begins.

Every school year the breadth of our engagement narrows. It starts with the physical: if it involves using your hands to do anything other than write or type, it goes. (Yes, we get the luxury of an hour or so of Phys Ed, but it's regarded almost as a 'gift' of free time.) The science people lose the chance to pursue the humanities, and vice versa. We are directed into channels where like minds learn and work together. Our former classmates with different aspirations, skill sets and worldviews disappear from our learning environment. Every time a subject we could learn about is taken away, a little of our flexibility of mind is stolen too. By the time I got to my final year of secondary school I was down to a set of closely aligned subjects, which severely limited the career paths I could take. For me it was Economics, Accounting, Legal Studies, English and Maths. My science days were over, the system had decided, which was a real shame. It wasn't until I was much older that I discovered an unrealised passion for science.

The higher we climb up the pyramid of learning the deeper we delve into selected subjects, but the more limited our worldview becomes. If there is one thing people need during times of dramatic societal and economic change, it's exposure to different possibilities and an open mind to a variety of disciplines, especially when previously siloed industries and worlds start to intersect, as they are today.

WHILE IT IS GOOD TO LEARN HOW TO DO SOMETHING, IT IS MORE VALUABLE TO KNOW HOW TO GET THINGS DONE.

Tasks are tactical; skills are temporary and maybe even disposable. Knowing how to do things can be outsourced, offshored and even automated. Narrow learning ignores the fact that understanding and working the system itself have infinitely more value and longevity.

The paperwork

Most degrees focus entirely on qualifying the student to pursue a certain career path. Over the past 200 years of the industrial era we have become a society of deeply ingrained formalisation. If you want to do something, you need to be selected and qualified, which means you need the piece of paper hanging on the wall, the stamp of approval, the ticket to enter the arena. Everywhere we go, everything we have and everything we do requires some form of paperwork to prove our entitlement or identity.

We are people of the certificate. The very first document in our life is the physical birth certificate that proves who we are and where we belong. We'll often protect and cherish this document, almost as though its loss would mean we ourselves would cease to be. When we meet others, cross borders and do business we present papers that prove who we are and our legitimacy. We belong because someone in a position of power has granted us this authority. The papers we accrue tell others that we deserve to be here, that we passed the legitimacy test.

Among the most important documents in our economic lives are our trade and academic certificates. If you want to be an accountant, the Certified Practising Accountant certificate authenticates that you have the required degree covering prerequisite subjects. Similar documents are required by prospective lawyers, medical practitioners and engineers. This is a good thing, which we shouldn't seek to change any time soon. Demanding that people doing any kind of work that has a direct impact on our health, safety and finances be appropriately qualified will remain essential in the kind of world I want to live in. However, there are many careers and jobs where formal qualifications may be desirable but are probably unnecessary. Every now and again some ambitious entrepreneurial person manages to sneak through the entry barriers without the requisite papers — a marketing director, chief architect, historian, graphic designer or app developer, for example. Sure, there are exceptions where formal authorisation continues to rule, as it should, but the list of jobs for which legitimate certification is indispensable is short. It would include: doctor, lawyer, physical therapist, optometrist, dentist, nurse, accountant, structural engineer, pharmacist, teacher, pilot ... and of course most trades, though even here we can learn on the job while we study without the need for tertiary schooling.

It is easy to see why formal qualification for a career that didn't really require it became the norm, as it was then the only way we could vet people. If you weren't formally qualified, then where would you pick up the knowledge? Accessing much of the knowledge and skills might be impossible or at least difficult. You might go to the library to read up on the subject, but employers would have no way of verifying what you actually knew. Let's say you managed to become skilled in a certain area, skilled enough to know as much as someone who studied it at university; you'd still have little chance of displaying this knowledge. How would the staff hirer be able to justify choosing a skilled applicant who lacked formal accreditation over a less impressive candidate with the requisite papers?

This is where the internet comes in. Not only has it become a vast resource through which we can learn almost anything; importantly, it has also become a place to display our own abilities and knowledge. The internet itself can become a CV generator. Simply type any person's name into Google and you'll soon find their qualifications, whether they were acquired formally or through practical experience.

In his book *The Inevitable*, Kevin Kelly writes of our society as having lived inside the culture of the book, valuing things only inasmuch as they were ratified by the authority of authors of the written word. Our world, he suggests, was 'a culture of expertise. Perfection achieved "by the book". Laws were compiled into official tomes, contracts were written down, and nothing was valid unless put into words on pages ... the heartbeat of

Western culture was turning pages of a book.' Today, though, 'most of us have become People of the Screen'.

In the past a piece of paper and mock-portfolio (developed in a classroom setting) that authenticated someone's visual arts degree would determine their chances of landing a role as a creative director. Now prospective employers are more likely to check out our YouTube channel, sampled and proved in the real world, to see what we have actually done. What would once be impossible to display to the market is now both easily accessed and more valued than the qualifications without which it would have once been impossible to get that gig.

THE GOOD NEWS FOR ALL IS THAT WHILE THE PAPERWORK WAS PERMANENT, THE SCREEN IS MALLEABLE – WE CAN MANIPULATE IT IN OUR FAVOUR.

Formal now or formal later?

Adult education has been a bastion for the comeback kid for a long time. For many people who lacked the maturity, desire, staying power or passion to study in their youth, night school can provide a kind of career salvation. It's not surprising that many decide to study later in life and have a second crack at getting that vital piece of paper. Time is sometimes the missing ingredient when it comes to our performance in the education system. For some reason we've all been judged as if we are a litre of milk with a use-by date, as if all our formal education needs to be squeezed in before some notional date stamped on the side of our heads, usually based on that birth certificate. It's a basic physiological fact that people develop at different speeds. We learn to walk and talk at different times, we reach puberty at different stages, and we reach our maximum height at different ages. But when it comes to school we all have no choice but to develop according to the steady, inflexible, linear timetable set by the system.

Post-school, informal learning has been how I reinvented my own future.

As a teenage boy, being accepted by my friends was way more important to me than academic achievement. I remember being excited by the prospect of learning to speak Italian at secondary school. Knowing another language would be so cool, I thought. I was so keen I studied the first chapter on my own in the summer before school started that year. But when I finally got to that first Italian class, my classmates were uninterested. They were indifferent to the point of disruption and even ridiculed the teacher. For me it was a new school. I knew only two other kids from my primary school, so I was entirely focused on fitting in. At that age, being accepted and having friends is all-important, a basic survival mechanism programmed deep in our DNA. So instead of following my original intention of diving deep into Italian, I followed the other boys mucking up the class. I squandered the opportunity to learn, and eventually dropped the subject. What a waste.

We can all probably remember something similar to my Italian experience from our immature years. A time when we really wanted to do something, but the social pressure to conform driven by the schoolyard mentality stole the opportunity from us. The shame is that most of us don't get a second chance at that lost opportunity, often because new pressures, financial and otherwise, emerge when we become adults.

I, however, did get a second chance to learn Italian. I had to: I mean, going around with a surname like mine and not knowing how to speak the language — it was downright embarrassing. So when I met my now wife (who could speak several languages, while I only had English under my belt) I was finally inspired to take action. I decided to go to night school and have another go. It's ironic that the same motivation that stopped me from learning the language in the first time (acceptance by my peers) is what inspired me to try it a second time. I personally believe peer acceptance is the biggest influence on our entire lives. Our desire to fit in with those we care about is all powerful. This is why our social circle of influence matters so much. Business philosopher Jim Rohn proposes that we become the average of the five people we spend the most time with. The best thing we can do to change our outcomes is to change who we choose to spend time with. What's fantastic is that these days we can spend that time with the world's best thinkers, people we've never met ... but more on that in Part III, 'Reinvention'.

So at the ripe old age of 28 I decided to join other adult learners and registered at the Centre for Adult Education. I soon found out that all my fellow students had similar stories to share about how they missed their chance to learn the language the first time around. And dropping out earlier was far less about their ability than about their environmental influences. Being surrounded by a bunch of motivated people who were doing this by choice made all the difference. Instead of competing to be the class clown, we were collaborating to lift each other up and learn the language. It really was an incredible experience for me because it changed my trajectory in life. For the first time I believed it wasn't too late to do *anything*.

To be honest, though, it wasn't as if it came easy; I did more than turn up to the lessons — I put in a lot of effort. I studied an hour every day. I did all my homework, did extra vocab drills, listened to the Italian radio station, hired foreign movies. I even went to the local Italian restaurant to practise with real Italians. I tried as much as possible to use common sense to accelerate the learning process. It's wonderful what a little extra effort can do. I hacked the learning process by embracing as many informal ways of learning as possible.

But without the Centre for Adult Education, I wouldn't have had a starting point to take off from. This would present a problem for many people. I was lucky enough to have the money to be able to afford it. Adult education isn't cheap, in terms of money or time. It cost me around $500 for the term, which included tuition fees, books, car parking and a few hours after work once a week. This could be a tough ask for anyone running a family and paying a mortgage. And if you don't live in a major city, night-time education opportunities are a lot thinner on the ground. But the good news is that this was in 2002. And, oh my goodness, has the world changed in that time. If anyone is serious about learning a language today it doesn't cost a cent, and you can live anywhere — all you need is access to the net.

Here's what's different about learning a language today and the tools at our disposal. We can find free lessons at all levels presented by generous teachers on YouTube. We can use one of the many available apps, such as Duolingo, that turn learning from a chore into a fun game. We can follow native speakers on Facebook or Twitter, and improve through brevity and frequency, with the added advantage of learning current slang. We can read and comment on blogs to practise our written form. We can use the incredible, gob-smacking Google translation AI, not just for words but for turns of phrase and longer, beyond-good translations. We can make friends with people in other countries who want to learn English or our native language as a kind of trade; Skype is a great way to do this. We can watch kids' cartoons and other TV shows online in the language of our choosing. We can pop on a set of virtual reality goggles and interact with one of the many new language programs where you are not just engaged in the language intellectually but act it out, virtually immersed in the homeland of the language. We can switch our web browser or smartphone to the language we choose to speak so we are looking at and using the language up to 74 times a day.[5] Oh, and Siri is quite the linguist too, with 17 languages currently under her belt, which means she'll be able to ask you to repeat that again because she didn't quite get that, and for the first time, it'll be your fault!

Adult education used to be pretty hard to access. It was costly and location sensitive. In many ways it was a bit like retail: you had to hope they sold what you wanted where you lived. You had to be inside the walls to be able to get what you needed, but now the possibilities are virtually unlimited. In just over a decade learning a language has gone from a traditional, still formal classroom setting to something that's available, mostly for free, at a time and location of our choosing. And the good news is this is just one narrow example of what has quickly become true for just about any area of learning you can think of. This kind of opportunity has never been available before in the history of humanity.

Pull up your roots

For some reason we have this idea that our lot in life is fixed. We act like we are a tree, with roots that aren't just familial and social but physical. One of the most powerful things we can do is pull up our roots and go somewhere else. When life isn't giving us the nourishment we need, how about just changing location? It's what we have done as a species so well and for so long, but we have somehow forgotten this core advantage of adaptability. The company closes its doors and we search for another job where we are — we wait for it to come to us. The best advice I can give anyone is this: don't wait for it to come to you — go find it. Don't act like a tree waiting and hoping for rain, looking up to the sky in times of drought. Remember we have legs and not roots. We can move somewhere else that offers new opportunities and a more abundant ecosystem.

My new location started as a 15-minute drive from my lounge room to night-school class. Maybe you should pull up your roots and go somewhere different, with different people, to get a different experience and find new intellectual nourishment. If you are a bit shy, you can now do this virtually. From the comfort of your home you can instantly transport yourself anywhere in the world to any group of people with ideas and thinking you'd like to embrace. The first thing any of us need to do to start the change we want to see is to change location — physically or virtually. While it is possible for new thinking to create new actions, it is impossible for new actions not to create new thinking. Change places.

CHAPTER 3
The future is informal

We've already established that the number of careers requiring formal validation can be listed in a short paragraph, so it's worth taking a look at how the informal market is starting to shape our world economically. People with something to offer and a risk-is-good attitude are starting to get noticed and finally gaining respect in our world. Let's take one of the world's most famous living artists — Banksy. For the uninitiated, Banksy is a street artist from the UK. Given that much of Banksy's art has been created illicitly (he has commonly been accused of trespass and vandalism, for example), he has chosen to keep his true identity closely guarded. But ask someone on the street about him and at least they'll know who he is, which probably cannot be said for Gerhard Richter. There's something special about what Banksy does that can offer us clues as to where the world is going. We are quickly moving from a world where the formal hierarchy rules to one where you can pick your own rules.

Surprisingly, Banksy makes the list of the top 100 living artists (based on the total value of works sold), sitting comfortably at number 84 on the list.[6] Unlike most of his fellow artists, however, Banksy wasn't 'chosen' or legitimised by anyone as an artist — he picked himself. He didn't rise up through traditional channels of art appreciation. Starting out as a streetwise graffiti artist with something to say, a bit of humour and a rebellious determination, he would come to culture jam one of the most exclusionary businesses of all, showing us that there is more than one path to respect. His tool of choice was a spray can, something anyone can afford, his canvas the concrete walls and buildings of backstreet Bristol. He discovered early that by using stencils he could work much faster when 'improving' public property. He uses templates of other people's work then mashes them up to create his own provocative interpretations.

Banksy is reinventing an industry that hasn't changed all that much since the Renaissance. He's changed the location, the tools and the rules, and even subverted the idea of the price or value of art. While some of his art has fetched huge sums in secondary markets, a lot of his work is given away for free to the public, wherever the public happens to be.

If you look closely you find parallels between what Banksy does and the way the web has altered our mindset of how to do pretty much anything. Banksy is a model of tomorrow — a self-starting, self-selecting entrepreneur, embracing some basic tools to make something the market values. This isn't just some sideshow either. Melbourne, Australia, where I live, has such a strong culture of graffiti-style street art that we have allocated a number of inner-city laneways where street artists are encouraged to pursue their craft. The cool part is that street art is building its own micro-economy. Something that was once regarded as about as useful as a broken window, a cost to society with no redeeming up side, has turned out to be the opposite. Melbourne's back alleys have become an international tourist destination. Any day of the week you can see scores of tour guides showing visitors the multi-coloured delights that were once bleak brick and concrete walls. The cafés and bars in the district are thriving, and it's not uncommon to see wedding parties using this unique urban backdrop for their photo shoots. The district now challenges the National Gallery of Victoria as the busiest art destination of the city. Previously disenfranchised youth have a calling, and fringe dwellers have found a way to the front line. There's every chance that you too will have non-traditional skills that could become an economic engine for your life.

Discover the entrepreneur within

Looking deep into where things come from can help us understand what is possible. It's too easy for us to assume the people or communities we revere started out with some kind of special talent or unfair advantage that gave them the edge, when often they just bothered to try when we didn't. Today, Silicon Valley is viewed as the epicentre of modern entrepreneurship, and in many ways it feels like a realm beyond the reach of mere mortals. Variously driven by Stanford University alumni, the military industrial complex, venture capital and the birth of the micro-processor, it feels as though the pedigree of its inhabitants, past and present, places it out of our league. While all these factors were and are genuine influences, there's a less discussed factor that drives the entrepreneurial ethic in that economy.

In his book *From Counterculture to Cyberculture*, author Fred Turner uncovers a deeper story behind how Silicon Valley emerged as the centre of the digital revolution. Many of the digital denizens who started the first online collectives were born out of the sixties hippie culture, a culture in which sharing and collaborative structures were valued above hierarchical and formal ones. They believed that the tools of the evil cold war institutions could be used for very different, altruistic purposes that would, in effect, subvert the interests of those who actually built much of the technology.

These utopian visionaries also had a deeply ingrained entrepreneurial mindset. Being outsiders without financial backers, they had to 'bootstrap' their own organisations. Many of them had spent time in communes and on the land where they had embraced the principles of self-sufficiency, cooperatives, mini supply chains, building off the grid, growing organic food, and selling and marketing their own wares. They also had a deep understanding of media and how to generate attention for alternative views; they had meetups and events where they recruited like minds. They were, without realising it, entrepreneurs in training.

Out of this unique confluence of ingredients something completely new would emerge. And while it was decades in the making, the mindset of not accepting the status quo, using emerging tools in new and interesting ways, and enthusiastically launching new projects created the perfect storm whose effects we see today in and around San Francisco. It was much more than the technology — it was the attitude of those who first accessed it.

Stewart Brand first published the iconic counterculture compendium the *Whole Earth Catalog* in 1968, modelling it on his and others' ideas of new collaborative social structures from the commune scene. In 1984 he produced an online version, the *Whole Earth 'Lectronic Link* (the WELL), which was perhaps the first open-source, available-to-anyone internet forum. It offered a discussion board where people could share information and knowledge in a way the world had never seen. It was, in real terms, the precursor to the hyperlinked World Wide Web. Brand famously declared that the computer was 'the new LSD' and a 'tool for transformation'. In a way he was right. We can use it to open our minds to possibilities in unimaginable ways. The connection to knowledge our devices provide offers an unmatched opportunity for anyone wishing to reshape their life — without having to ask anyone for permission. No one ever has had the opportunity we have today to invent our own future, but we need the courage to find the entrepreneur buried deep inside of us.

Self-reliance needs a comeback

'People have careers; companies have jobs.' A colleague once told me this during my linear corporate years when I was feeling on the outer with my manager at the time. Before this insight I had always had a false idea that we had a career with a company, that the all-powerful organisation held our petty little future in their hands. I finally worked out why many of us worry so much about how we are perceived in the marketplace. It's because the entrepreneurial spirit has been stolen from our hearts. Sometime during the process of becoming structured industrial automatons, we lost the art of self-reliance.

**WE ARE BORN NATURAL ENTREPRENEURS
WITH A CREATIVE, ARTISTIC AND SALES MINDSET,
THEN SCHOOL INVESTS 12 YEARS
IN DELIBERATELY ERASING IT.**

Before we left the farms and villages to pursue the relative prosperity of factory labour, most of us were independent workers. We were craftspeople, smiths, carpenters, share farmers. We had trades, mostly worked outside of an organisational construct and belonged to workers' guilds. We were independent workers who traded our skills for payment. We didn't draw a wage or a salary; we had customers. I'm not talking about the customers who walk into a retail store, who discover you through search engine optimisation or who you call with the name of a big brand behind you to sell them something they already buy. I'm talking about the real ones you have to win and serve yourself.

When we build up a stock of personal customers, we find our financial survival relies on an additional skill set. We become small business people, micro-preneurs able to turn our hand to much more than any course could teach us. We need to be able to sell direct, manage cash flows, balance the books, manage the supply chain of raw materials, invest time and money in upskilling ourselves, and master new tools as they arrive. When things go sour and business is not doing well, we need to be able to spot it ourselves and react fast. We must be self-reliant from end to end. We'll notice a poor crop yield or a drop-off in the number of customers as it is occurring. A fall in our personal income from the farm or craft shop would inspire us to take action, to change. We manage our own situation pre-emptively to fix things, to fill in skill gaps, to pivot to other sources of income. There is no leave without pay, no redundancy. There's only self-reliance. In the real world, everyone doesn't get a trophy.

Maybe the loss of these skills explains why so many people have such low financial literacy, why their personal finances are a mess. When we add to this the marketing chicanery practised by most financial institutions to trick consumers, it's no wonder we live in such a debt-laden society.

Before the industrial revolution a very small percentage of people were waged or salaried employees. While reliable statistics are difficult to find, some reports suggest a figure as low as 10 per cent. Today the numbers are reversed. In Australia a little over 10 per cent of those undertaking paid employment work for themselves. There are, however, some signs that this trend is starting to turn, with more people seeking out independent income sources again. This could be because people are struggling to find reliable employment, or it could be that new freelance and startup opportunities are being driven by technology. A recent study[7] found that self-employment is at its highest rate in the UK for the past 40 years, at 15 per cent. For context, the figure reached a low of 8.7 per cent in 1975, when the country was at the peak of its industrial power before low-cost labour markets and Asian manufacturing started to undermine its manufacturing sector. If there was ever a time to shift your focus towards leveraging your own resources and unique skill set, then that time is now. You will be early and ahead of the curve, but for the observant the trend can already be recognised.

The pace of change is super-radical

As we make the shift from being people of the book to people of the screen (you're probably reading this on a screen or listening to it on a device), the pace of change continues to accelerate. I'm not talking about the explosion of technology or computing power; here I'm referring to the *liquidity* of information. It seems as though everything we even think these days is published almost immediately, exchanged in the marketplace of liquid information. Pixels stream down into our devices, which overnight can change what was true yesterday. Those who want to know about a technical innovation or research finding can do so almost instantly. Our ability to connect means information transfers at the speed of light, and this has another impact.

Being connected means we have access to more cognitive ingredients more quickly. As these ideas are exchanged, every iteration happens faster, and this causes a problem for formal education providers. It is difficult for any syllabus in a structured environment simply to keep up. To be truly informed, we have to seek out the informal. We have to be at the meetups where those inventing the future hang out. We have to be curious enough about the work we choose to seek out those reshaping it. We have to look to the fringe. But more importantly, we need to be curious enough to explore seemingly unrelated pieces of information from divergent spaces. The spaces we care about, which may at first seem unrelated, can now be put together in new and interesting ways. Our unique experience and perspective on life will create our own personal economic advantage.

No one has the unique set of collective experiences you have, and the way you bring those to the market is where the gold lies. In a digital world, we all engage with the same factors of production, the 1's and 0's of the digital world, but we don't share the same life pattern. The particular path that got each of us here is our unique value proposition. It's vital we embrace our ability to learn informally and to match that learning with what we experience. In the real world there is no red pen to tell us we're wrong and remind us of the mistakes that are best avoided. In the real world we don't have to attribute our ideas to their original sources, as we did in school.

It's time to just make stuff up again

No, not the news, or your own facts. But what you can do and how to go about doing it. Watch a five-year-old kid play for half a day and you'll see levels of creativity that'll blow your mind. They have an incredible ability to 'make things up'. And they gain immediate feedback from the market — the other kids they're playing with, who will soon let them know if they like the ideas or games they are proposing. But as adults we have it back to front. We've convinced ourselves that our ideas and opinions don't matter much. I remember being told when writing essays at school that I had to quote from other people's work, and how weird that felt. Why couldn't I just write what I thought? Why did the ideas and views I expressed, in any area other than science, still have to be drawn from someone else's? Why did what others thought matter more than what I thought? To be taken seriously we are expected to reference where we get our ideas from, whether it's another person's work or some research proving things are the way we say they are. While this is important in science, it's generally not true for making a living. The opposite is true: everything of value is being created by us now, today. So long as what we do is in the bounds of legality, we should be literally 'making up' as much stuff as possible.

The trick they pulled on us, persuading us to not conceive of original ideas, to not create anything new and to keep our opinions to ourselves, is rapidly losing its power. And this gets me excited.

WE ALL STILL HAVE THE ABILITY TO JUST 'MAKE THINGS UP'. NOW WE HAVE ACCESS TO THE TOOLS TO CREATE ANYTHING; NOW THE ECONOMY IS BEING TOTALLY REDESIGNED, WE JUST NEED TO FORGET WHAT WE WERE TOLD AND TO START FORMING OUR OWN OPINIONS AND CREATING SOMETHING NEW.

And when someone says, 'That's cool. Where'd you get the idea for that?' you can proudly reply, 'I just made it up'. Find the child inside.

The formal institutions really don't get it

When I was bootstrapping my first dotcom startup, I was living skinny on minimal income. I was investing a fair amount of time and money in it, and needed some supplementary income, so I wanted to get some extra paid work that wouldn't interfere with my entrepreneurial endeavours. I found out that you don't have to have a PhD to lecture at a university; all you need is a bachelor's degree and experience in the area you want to teach in. So I got this gig tutoring various marketing subjects. With no formal training as a teacher, I just put my heart into it. I took what I knew about doing real marketing and the principles I studied at university, and I made it up. Sure, I stuck to the syllabus, but I made up what I thought would be a good way to pass on what the kids needed to know. I took examples from the real world, and gave them homework they could relate to, with brands they knew well. Many students later told me it was the best class they had taken in their three years of study.

For four years I tutored a number of marketing-related subjects to first-, second- and third-year students. I really enjoyed it and wanted to be the best at it. I've always loved the idea of teaching, but I never liked how little teachers earn — firstly, because it's among the most important jobs there is in our society; and secondly, because it is very difficult to do well. I was desperate to get a gig doing some lectures as well. This was largely the domain of the PhDs and permanent staff, but I did get some opportunities. I would do fill-in jobs on a semi-regular basis, and again I smashed it. I'd have a crowd around me after every lecture.

All this is not to impress you, but so what I'm about to tell you makes sense. You need to understand that the people making decisions about your future in your company or industry, or whatever walk of life you happen to play in economically, don't know nearly as much as you think they do. In fact, if you're good, or have potential, they are probably scared you may disrupt their way of life. They may see you as some kind of threat, especially if you're not 'one of them', if you didn't progress through the formal channels or come from their world.

So after I'd been getting paid by the university for a number of years, delivering incredible service to their customers — the students — I found out they were going to offer a new unit, Entrepreneurialism, in which students would learn how to get a startup up and running. This was when universities around the world were starting to look seriously at the area. I was pumped, convinced it was the perfect subject for me to take a lead on. I've always enjoyed talking, sharing ideas and holding an audience's attention. I really love teaching. There is nothing more wonderful than sharing ideas with others — it's a pure gift for both parties. So I set up a meeting with the *decision maker* on who the lecturer would be. The university knew I was generating a real buzz among the students.

I made my pitch on why I should take on the new subject, how I'd develop the course content and deliver the lectures and tutorials to leave the kids totally inspired. I went through my history as an entrepreneur: my first startup at age 11 — an organic egg farm; two successful exits where I had sold my own companies; and the past few years studying and comparing startups and big companies. I was at that time building a web startup that had become a local media darling. I was a living, breathing entrepreneur with something to give. Here is what they told me.

'I know you can do it. I know you'd be the best possible teacher of this subject for our students. But I can't let you do it. I have to give it to one of my "researchers".'

I found it curious that they used the word *researcher* instead of *teacher* or *lecturer*. They told me these days it was all about getting papers published. I later found out that the lecturer they chose had never run a startup and was a career academic. It was pretty much like learning from a scientist who had never been in a lab. I can still see the decision maker's face, and the comments are carved inside my brain for ever. It's actually kind of cathartic writing it here. I'm not saying it was anyone's fault. Organisations have their own processes and objectives, and often people are constrained to make decisions based on what their superiors want. I've worked in enough large companies to know that.

So, a great reminder for anyone who ever had a door closed in their face: there's a very good chance it isn't about your ability. It's absolutely vital we don't let it kill our spirit when it happens to us. Don't ever let anyone block you from doing what you want to do. Just keep forging ahead and knocking on doors until they open. And if you keep knocking they *will* open in the end, and when they do, the person inside will appreciate your work and effort more than those who didn't want you. Just think of it as a process of self-selection, of finding the right people for you.

I did end up getting a quasi-lecturing job — actually one that's much better than the position at the university would have been. On the back of my previous book, *The Great Fragmentation*, I am often invited to do keynote speeches on the future of business and technology. I get paid extremely well to do it and those who hire me (mostly large corporations facing disruption) appreciate the real-world experience I have in the startup sector, as well as the stuff I've literally *made up*. And it comes with a number of bonuses the university could never have provided, including travel around the world and enough free time to continue to write and to build new startup businesses, both of which ensure that my lectures only get better as I generate new ideas and fresh content. It's a kind of virtuous circle, another reminder that it's vital we know and believe that the 'No's' often lead to better 'Yes's' later.

Definitions really matter

How smart do you have to be successful? Before we can answer this question it's important we define a couple of these words, because quite frankly most people are walking around with incorrect definitions of both 'successful' and 'smart'.

Success is an internal measure. It's something we have to define for ourselves, based on personal desires and goals; it's a relative measure of where we want to end up as against where we started. This is why I get frustrated when I hear people talk about someone else's success. They see an ex-colleague drive past in a Porsche, or appear on TV, and say, 'Gee, he's really successful!' My initial response is 'How do you know?' We can only ever measure success against the objectives we set for ourselves. Certain financial rewards may spell success to them, but they may not. There is nothing wrong with wanting money or fame, but they are just two possible measures of success from an infinite list. They may have other objectives they have yet to reach. They may be miserable, for all we know. While fame and perceived financial wealth are archetypal measures of success that society would have us believe in, the truly smart people in our society understand that happiness is the ultimate success, and there are many paths to achieving it. If anything, fame and fortune are more likely to find us when our goals are not limited to those two measures.

SUCCESS IS A CHOICE

Here's the best definition of success I've ever heard, from Earl Nightingale in 1956: 'Success is the progressive realization of a worthy ideal.' There is just so much gold in that short sentence that it is worth breaking it down.

- » *Progressive:* It's a path, an undertaking. It may be a destination but isn't necessarily one. It's the start that really matters. It reminds us that the having is in the doing.

- » *Realization:* We don't give up. We keep on trying until we get there.

- » *Worthy:* The goal itself isn't enough. It's got to deserve our time and effort, to be something worth doing, for ourselves and hopefully for our community or society. It should take us forward emotionally and even morally. If generating money is one of the objectives, fine, and in a modern economy that certainly matters, but we don't limit ourselves to that.

It turns out success is more about effort than anything else; we all know this intuitively. We know how good anything feels when we really have tried our best; it can be more satisfying than a victory that comes too easily or for which we just got lucky. It's the undertaking that nourishes the soul. This is why when we think back to the great things we've experienced in our life they are generally moments and not things. The times we spent with people, the laughter, the meetings, the travel, the pride after completing a project. Even when we bought that expensive 'thing' we wanted as an adult or even as a teenager, the reason it felt so good was we probably had to work hard to get it. It is the satisfaction we value; the thing is really just a reflection of what we've done. It's okay to chase money, but the why is always more important, the driver that makes it all worth it. Money for money's sake is often a false flag.

When it comes to the financial side of success there is a simple rule I follow that helps me sleep at night: it is okay to accumulate money so long as it is done in the service of the many and not at the expense of the many. This is a great sense test of what we are doing. It makes it so easy to recognise if the project is 'worthy' of pursuing. Once we pass this little mental challenge, we can have our financial cake and eat it too.

YOU'RE SMARTER THAN YOU THINK

Now we know the true meaning of success, let's have a look at smart. The usual, incorrect definition relates it to 'intellectual horsepower'. As you can probably guess, my definition has little to do with the intellectual gymnastics we get judged on at school. It isn't about our mind's raw potential. I can't even capture it in a sentence, as I did with success, but I can provide some guidance to what makes someone smart. The easiest way to do this is first to give you a list of things that do *not* show how smart someone is.

So let's start with the old-school favourite: IQ, which quite frankly is a terrible measure of smarts. IQ tests are really only good at determining how good someone is at taking IQ tests. The fact that they can be gamed in order to improve your score is very telling. I once bought a book on how to improve my IQ. It contained a number of exercises to practise to get your score up. I managed to lift mine up 25 points, which illustrates that IQ is really a kind of intellectual sprint. With practice we can improve it, but a high IQ matters little in life unless you're pursuing a particular intellectual endeavour.

Another thing we can cross off the list is how fast we can do things. Sure, it's nice to be able to work something out quickly, put together pieces and make sense of something ahead of others, but it's not often a necessity of life. This is again that finish-line, time-based ethic from the factory coming in to influence our definitions. Let's take the three-hour exam. Now when did you ever do anything in life, outside of a sporting competition or time-based test, where the time mattered that much.

PEOPLE SO OFTEN CONFUSE DAILY DEADLINES AND FORGETTABLE TASKS WITH SLOW, CONSISTENT BEHAVIOURS, WHICH HAVE A BIGGER IMPACT ON IMPROVING OUR LIVES.

Everything important I've ever done took days, months, even years to complete. We need to remove completion time from our definition of smarts. All that mentality will do for us is provide false comparisons that may lead us to quit sooner than we should.

Here I'll add something to the list that smart people don't do: they don't waste opportunity. They don't waste things like the various natural talents they have, and everyone has natural gifts. They don't waste the opportunities offered by their direct environment. They don't waste the time they have. Time is one of life's great equalisers. No matter how much time someone feels they need, by any measure they'll never find more than 24 hours in a day. How they use it is what's important. Smart people don't waste money either. Money ought to be spent, enjoyed, shared and invested, but not in a careless fashion. Smart people use their money in a considered way. All money is allocated somewhere, so the choices we make are important, and anyone can learn to do this better than 90 per cent of the population. More on this in Part II, 'Revenue'.

Smart people choose to use all their abilities, including their natural gifts. Smart people take advantage of the small advantages they have and build on them, step by step, as if they are making advantage deposits that will compound over time. Smart people are lifelong learners. Smart people know how to combine what they've learned; whether the source of the lessons is books, work or life, they aren't afraid to mash them up into something that just makes sense for them. Above all, they are practical. Smart people are long-game players, not sprinters. Even if their core skills have some kind of fast-twitch capacity to them, they know to focus on leveraging them for long-term advantage. I've met very bright people who for some reason are not interested in using their potential. On the flipside, I've met many people of average intelligence who have done amazing things that you might assume could only be done by a brilliant person. It turns out that brilliance is about using what you have, which is usually enough, to do something really bright.

Smart people generally display the qualities we value in humans: honesty, integrity, kindness, generosity, empathy and good humour, to name a few.

Finally, being smart is about using what's available to you to achieve your own objectives in life, not someone else's. Your worthy ideal can be as simple or as complex as you please.

Smarts are relative. They depend on how we use the potential we've been given to achieve personal objectives. They're about utilisation. In the end, we all know that being less than we can be chips away at the soul.

So here's my attempt at a definition:

BEING SMART MEANS USING YOUR ABILITIES TO MAXIMISE THE POTENTIAL FOR HAPPINESS FOR YOURSELF AND OTHERS.

MY SCHOOL REPORT

Now here's a glimpse of a variety of my own school reports from secondary school (see figure 3.1). Yes, there are some embarrassing truths about me, but my aim here is simply to demonstrate how little our formal school results matter, and how average people can do well in our world.

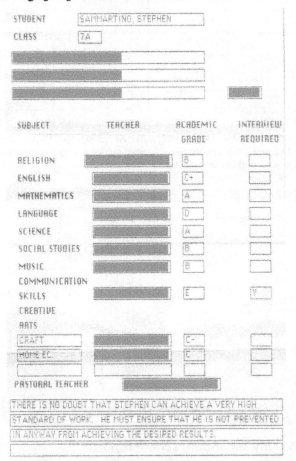

Year 7: I entered my first year of high school with my desire intact, and got A's and B's. Big misses in language (Italian) and, ironically, communication skills. As I mentioned earlier, I was discouraged by peer groups in these subjects.

Figure 3.1: My secondary school reports *(Continued)*

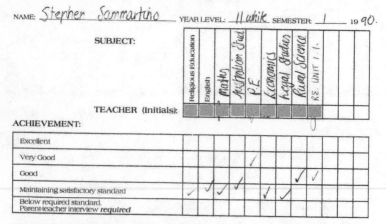

NAME: *SAMMARTINO STEPHEN* YEAR LEVEL: *9* TERM: *3*

SUBJECT	RELIGIOUS EDUCATION	ENGLISH	MATHEMATICS	SCIENCE	SOCIAL STUDIES	COMMERCE	TYPING	FRENCH	ITALIAN	PHYS. ED.	CR. ARTS 1	CR. ARTS 2	
TEACHER (Initials)													
ACHIEVEMENT													
Excellent													
Very Good		✓	✓										
Good	✓						✓			✓			
Maintaining satisfactory standard	✓				✓	✓					✓		
Slightly below required standard							✓		✓				
Considerably below required standard–having difficulty													

Year 9: By now the system was wearing me down, as were my 'mates' — the decline had started. (You'll notice they changed grades A-E to Excellent to Unsatisfactory. All part of the self esteem movement).

NAME: *Stephen Sammartino* YEAR LEVEL: *11 white* SEMESTER: *1* 19 *90*.

SUBJECT:	Religious Education	English	Maths	Australian Stud	P.E.	Economics	Legal Studies	Rural Science	RE. UNIT 1.1.			
TEACHER (Initials):												
ACHIEVEMENT:												
Excellent												
Very Good					✓							
Good				✓				✓	✓			
Maintaining satisfactory standard	✓	✓	✓	✓		✓	✓					
Below required standard. Parent-teacher interview *required*												

Year 11: By the 5th year of high school, the system wasn't working for me. I'm now failing subjects I used to excel at.

Figure 3.1: My secondary school reports

As you can see I'm no scholar. Anyone with an average intellectual capability — for our purposes, let's define that as the ability to read and comprehend — can become smart enough to build an extraordinary life.

Everything important I know in life, everything that created and shaped my living today (excluding the ability to read and write), I have taught myself. It's important we follow the advice of Mark Twain (channelling an earlier novelist, Grant Allen) and 'don't let schooling interfere with our education'. The etymology of the word education has all the clues we need: the Latin verb *educare* means to draw out, bring up or rear. As we would a child. Our education is about our ability to learn and grow, to be able to deduce things from the world around us. It's not about how long we've spent sitting at a desk in a room among rows of other obedient, often bored fellow students.

CHAPTER 4
The future of work

Change isn't just happening fast, it's skyrocketing. While we're constantly told that the pace of change is accelerating, it's hard for our brains to comprehend exponential change. The human mind is local and linear. Even when we are told a change is exponential, we are likely to underestimate its impact. Here's my favourite example: Imagine taking 32 linear steps forward. If you did this, you'd advance around 32 metres. If you took the same number of steps but doubled the length of each step, you'd circumnavigate the Earth 54 times (travelling 2.2 million kilometres).

The reason this is important is that most of the technologies we work with today are advancing exponentially. They double in power and/or efficiency every 18 to 24 months, and this influences the types of tools we use and the world we live in. In grade school maths, exponentials are often introduced as a fun mathematical curiosity. We trot out an example like the one above to show how quickly things expand, to marvel at it, and then we move past it. But it's actually among the most important mathematical principles of our time, because it impacts the technology we connect with and use every day, and how we earn our money. Rather than going through all the different technologies that follow this law of accelerating returns — smartphones, drones, driverless cars, network speed and data storage, to name a few — let me give you this instead: Imagine that every single thing that relies on digital technology will be twice as efficient and powerful in 18 months' time.

Think of the current voice-activated digital assistants such as Siri, Cortana, Alexa and Google Voice Search. Siri is now five years old and is, well, about as intelligent as a 10-year-old. But in five years from now Siri won't be a bit brighter — equivalent to, say, a 15-year-old (that's linear thinking). She'll be a genius who is smarter than every person in the world. She'll have a PhD in every subject, with the ability to understand everything humans know and more. This is the world we're living in, right now.

Your job is already gone

The future of work is not a job. It's arguable that the glory days of structured jobs are already behind us, and that in the future very few of us will have jobs as we know them today. In fact, your job is already gone — its time just hasn't elapsed yet. Humans have a funny way of inventing the future they imagine. We think of things, then subconsciously we find a way to make them happen. It's a bit like a form of collective sentience. If we think something will happen, we tend to move towards it. There are two main reasons why your job, and mine, are about to disappear: the first is artificial intelligence; the second is the move back to a world of independent workers — freelancers and entrepreneurs. So let's tackle the scariest of these first, AI.

Until now it has been mainly labourers and blue-collar workers who have been displaced by automation. But now, for the first time, white-collar workers and even management are facing displacement. Even those occupations with the highest qualifications and societal respect are not immune. Robots replacing surgeons — yep. Tricorders replacing doctors — done. Legal apps replacing lawyers — check. Just as we once delegated much of our physical heavy lifting to machines powered by fossil fuels, we will increasingly entrust our 'smartness' to artificial intelligence. Jobs dominated by left-brain logic will be outsourced to AIs. If there is a cost advantage in using machinery, corporations and governments will take it.

It's easy to worry about the impact of AI on our economic futures. A recent report from the Committee for Economic Development of Australia[8] estimates that 40 per cent of jobs that currently exist in Australia have a moderate to high likelihood of disappearing within the next 10 to 15 years due to technological advancements. These types of predictions are being replicated the world over, especially in developed nations whose labour forces tend to be service oriented. They are the research fear generator du jour, but they rarely mention why this is something we could choose to be positively excited about. Because maybe we can actually replace these obsolete jobs and do something better with our days. A 2016 World Economic Forum report on the future of jobs[9] gives us a clue to this by forecasting that around 65 per cent of children starting primary school today will end up working in jobs that don't yet exist. As someone with children just entering primary school I couldn't be more delighted, because it means we might finally stop pushing kids prematurely down a narrow career path. It means we need to teach our kids the core skills of adaptability, flexibility and tackling people's and society's real problems, not simply training for jobs. But first we must face up to the reality that the world of work is going to change dramatically.

Yes, the robots will take your job, but there aren't that many bison hunters around anymore! All jobs are eventually displaced or changed by technology. Technology-driven unemployment has always been a fixture of the human experience. Look at the history of labour, which I like to sum up in just four words: spear, seed, spanner and silicon. At every stage of human evolution, new tools (automation, in a sense) have revolutionised the way we approach old tasks and introduced new tasks. Our challenge is to make the most of the tools we have. Hunters were judged on their success in bringing home food. Successful farmers made the best use of agricultural tools and methods to increase their yield. We will be judged by how well we work with the AIs. As they take over more and more of the tasks around us I'm certain there will be many jobs we won't miss at all. Fifty years from now some of these jobs will have come to be regarded as human rights violations. The dirty, the dangerous and the disrespected roles will be outsourced to 'non-humans', and that will be good for humanity.

Technology has always been a net job creator. People worried what we'd do when we all left the farm, but we found an alternative, and it improved our living standards dramatically. The truth is, the media's main source of fuel is fear, and promoting the positive side of change doesn't generate the same level of interest that scare-mongering does. In evolutionary terms too, we are programmed to pay more attention to danger than to joy. Our current operating system — the Human OS — is more than 200 000 years old. It had to make sense of a complex and dangerous world, so it developed short cuts or biases for certain situations. The most common bias is towards prioritising potentially negative situations over positive ones. This kept us alive in the early days, just as today it keeps pessimistic news and clickbait alive. We can't help but pay attention, 'just in case'.

Here, as a mind jam to counter the bad news, are some recently created jobs that no one is writing economic reports on:

UX Designer, App Developer, Drone Operator, Crowdfunding Advisor, Smartphone Game Developer, Blogger, Podcaster, Social Media Specialist, Wikipedia Moderator, Content Curator, Community Manager, Uber Driver, Airbnb Host,

Web Videographer, YouTube Content Creator, eBook Publisher, Bitcoin Trader, Bitcoin Miner, Blockchain Specialist, E-Commerce Consultant, SEO Specialist, Genetics Counsellor, Sustainability Advisor, Citizen Journalist, MOOCs Tutor, Big Data Analyst, Cloud Services Specialist, Robot Ethicist, Privacy Consultant, IoT Privacy Specialist, Snapchat Marketing Agency, Virtual Reality Retailer, Drone Delivery Operator.

This list is just a small sample set from my perspective, and there are a hundred variants to each of these. I'm sure your industry experience or worldview means you could expand the list vastly. There are just under 10 million app developers in the world today, with more than 800 000 more starting up every year. A job that didn't exist before the smartphone.

The crazy thing about these 'new jobs' is they are all learnable, mostly for free. All you need is (1) the ability to read and (2) an internet connection. While some of them sound complex, I've specifically chosen activities that don't require exceptional mathematical ability or scientific knowledge, just the will to learn and put in the effort. And no, the government or your boss won't save you or pay you to learn any of them. No one can do your push-ups for you, but if you make the effort, the rewards are there. The new jobs, and more importantly the *business opportunities* around them, are there for the taking, and they'll often pay more than your old job did. One of my favourite facts is that UX designers earn as much as and sometimes more than software engineers.

A UX (User Experience) designer, as you'd expect, designs the end-to-end experience the user will have with a product or service. This often involves visual design for screen-based interactions. What's interesting is how in demand this type of work is and how easy (by which I mean 'human') the learning process is. Most people, with a moderate amount of concentrated effort, can learn. But the cool thing is, the non-technical nature of this job that mostly lives within the tech industry means the barriers to entry are relatively low. The best UX designers I've met haven't been the best techs, but rather the most empathic. The technical side of the work can be learned in a reasonably short time, and the demand for candidates for this often high-paying gig is only going to increase, especially when companies work out the competitive advantage it offers.

The choice is really between wishing the world was like yesterday or taking advantage of the opportunities today. Exactly zero is the number of future-proof jobs out there. From bison hunter to binary coder, they all eventually succumb to human progress. Structural unemployment is a permanent fixture in the human experience, and our best bet is to embrace the flux it creates.

THE MOST VALUABLE THING WE CAN DO, THEN, IS HAVE A MALLEABLE MINDSET — TO PARTICIPATE IN THE REINVENTION OF OURSELVES, AS MUCH AS THE WORLD AROUND US, TO REMEMBER THAT WE ARE THE CHANGE WE SEE.

Yes, the pace of change is scary, but it's never been more possible to upskill, reskill or new-skill. So next time you read a report on the impending doom of your industry, job or financial future, just remember that it is your decision how it will affect you.

An independent future

Imagine for a second a company in the future with zero employees. You might think this isn't possible, and I agree. There will always be non-routine, disparately linked tasks that humans can do, should do and will want to do given that corporations are invented by human beings. But we also know that a goal of most companies is to reduce their employee costs. So here's what we will see much sooner than we might imagine: a company with many people working for it, but none of them as official company employees.

This pattern is already clearly being established. We are quickly moving from a world of access instead of ownership. Many call it the sharing economy, but more accurately it is the rental economy. Renting is cheaper than owning. Historically, the level of friction associated with renting has been too high on many things, including workers, but technology has a way of removing friction, of liquefying assets and increasing their visibility and availability. People are choosing to access things instead of owning them. They've realised that most things they own are used for only a tiny fraction of the time. Excluding a house in which to store our belongings and a fridge, our most used asset in life is our bed, and at best it enjoys a 50 per cent utilisation ratio. The second most expensive thing we buy, a car, has a utilisation ratio as low as 10 per cent. Access rather than ownership has been a broadly established principle for houses, cars, music, books — you name it. If it is cheaper to access something when we need it, with all the benefits of ownership, then the shift to that structure is inevitable. Now corporations access people on demand. Employees are entering the rental space. In the future we'll be *projecteers* working on a number of projects for ourselves and for other companies, renting our core competency to the market as and when it is needed.

In this freelance world, employers will be able to pay people more because of the project orientation. They are interested in the value of the outcome of the project, and can pay based on that without taking into account the associated costs of 'owning' employees. They won't pay you during your downtime, and you won't waste your time because you'll be paid only on what you deliver. They don't have to invest in training (that's your job, but more on that in Part III, 'Reinvention'), and they don't have to pay out superannuation or 401k, medical insurance, overtime, annual leave, public holidays or redundancy, and you'll still be better off for it. How? Because you'll earn twice the rate you do now in half the time. Enough to cover all of these costs independently. There'll be startups emerging that take over these administrative tasks for us, providing group discounts at the corporate rate for a world of independent workers. The new format invents even more opportunities for entrepreneurs and freelancers alike doing tasks that corporations once did. In this world we can all focus on what we're actually here to do and outsource the rest.

It's comforting to remember that professionals who have historically rented themselves out directly to customers have always earned more than the majority of employees. Doctors, physiotherapists, accountants, dentists, plumbers and the like have always had the advantage of independence on their side. But now, as the friction is removed, all kinds of work can be done for corporations without working for them. And here's some extra good news for those renting their time to a large number of customers: if you are snubbed by one, no big deal, you're still in business — which significantly reduces life risk.

There is a platform orientation occurring in business life, a layer of information being built on the concrete and steel of our physical world — a *meta-structure*, if you like. Increasingly, we'll be dancing on information stages provided by others. Let's look at some examples of how this is already happening today:

» Smartphone app stores provide a platform for app developers and entrepreneurs of every type to dance on.

» Uber and Lyft provide a business-generating tool for drivers (at least until they're replaced by driverless vehicles).

» WordPress provides a platform for citizen journalists and 28 per cent of all sites on the World Wide Web.

» Spotify provides a platform for musicians, and YouTube for anyone wanting to publish content in video format.

» PayPal, Square and Stripe provide world-class payment platforms for anyone needing to transfer money over the web.

» The blockchain database provides a platform for smart contracts without centralised authority.

» Co-working spaces provide space for mobile freelancers to work from anywhere in the world.

» Freelancing websites such as 99designs, upwork.com and freelancer.com provide marketplaces for people to find the skills they need.

This is a tiny sample, and just the start, but we can look overseas to developing markets to see how this will play out. Markets without a legacy infrastructure tend to embrace the shifts in work structure more quickly because they don't have a powerful incumbent system to circumvent. Many, for example, go straight to mobile and wireless and may never have owned a PC or plugged into the internet. They too are embracing global freelance opportunities to arbitrage the higher wage scale in developed markets. We'll have no choice but to follow their lead if we don't want to be disrupted by developing countries.

These platforms for freelancers and entrepreneurs are made possible by a few key technological factors. The cost of tools is rapidly falling. Office equipment, for example, used to be incredibly expensive: photocopiers, laser printers, telecommunications, teleconferencing all came at great cost. Now they are either cheap or, in the smartphone wifi era, simply redundant. You can connect wherever you go. Then there is the reduced friction of finding people, or projecteers, to do the work required. Anyone we need is just a few clicks away, their skills, reputation and network all open sourced on the web.

Another force that is contributing to the trend towards independent work is the frequency with which we move around today. When I first entered the workforce, it looked bad if you didn't stay with a company for at least five years. Now they wonder what's wrong with you if you're still in the same place for two years. Today career fluidity and mobility are respected.

FREELANCING IS THE PERFECT STEPPING STONE TO A WORLD WHERE INDEPENDENCE IS THE NEW NORMAL.

It's a radical shift from the halcyon era of lifetime employment after World War II.

In developed markets, the new world order of technology firms, including but not limited to Apple, Alphabet, Amazon and Facebook, are very different from the old order as represented by the likes of Exxon, Ford, General Motors and General Electric. The new firms have a far lower number of employees per dollar of revenue. In mid 2019 Facebook had 39 651 employees[10] and a projected annual income of US$69 billion, or US$1.7 million per employee. Let's compare this to the Ford Motor Company. Ford currently have 199 000 employees and an income of US$67 billion, equating to just US$805 000 per employee. The pattern is clear to see, and Facebook's numbers are probably understated given they are overinvesting in growth markets. In the past the company provided the income source for the community; now the company provides opportunities for the community to create income from it.

This shift isn't coming sometime in the future; it's already well underway, and will continue to strengthen because the incentives for all parties point clearly to it. We are going back to the way things were, but this time we'll be digital craftspeople, working in and around the corporations, which didn't exist before the industrial era. Our personal brands, market awareness and ability to assess the change in skill requirements will be key to our success. We'll need to be able to spot the changes and then adapt to them. I firmly believe there will never be a world without work, because humans invent things to do, but during this time of technological upheaval we will have to change our mindset on where value will be created.

The labour escalator

A simple economic fact is that if a person has $100 in their wallet, it will always be allocated. In 1996 $10 of that $100 might have gone into getting a film developed. Now it goes elsewhere, maybe towards the monthly fee of a smartphone. The allocations change, and so does the work around those expenditure allocations, but the money will always be spent, saved or invested. If you want to be future proof, it's important to pay close attention to what your friends are spending their time and money on. Economic shifts always happen on the street before they hit Wall Street. Spending patterns and how people reallocate their available funds tells us so much, it's worth paying attention to; it's always where tomorrow's opportunities lie.

We need to imagine that human labour is a bit like an escalator. Every new job, industry or type of work that arrives steps onto the labour escalator for a period of time. The job or type of work remains on the escalator until we find a more efficient way of getting that task done, then the escalator just stops. Some of these tasks have been on the escalator for a very long time — like cooking and medical advice. Some escalators don't take people forward for long at all — like telephone switchboard operator, toll booth collector, lift operator or typist. Some of these gigs had less than 50 years of escalator time.

Imagine all these escalators are lined up next to one another, but they are all moving at different speeds. Some look like they may stop pretty soon. Some you can ride all the way to the end of your career, an option that used to be well respected. Some escalators get smaller as time goes by, so fewer people can fit on them. These are the ones you want to jump off as soon as you can. Our task is to seek out and jump onto other escalators with better prospects. To do this we can't treat it simply as a ride and just stand there; we need to work while we are on it, walk forward, look around us, get ready to make the leap across to another one. In the long run, we have to try to take ownership of an escalator, not just take a ride on it. But most of all, we shouldn't whinge when the escalator stops; we should always be able to tell when it is coming to a stop, and it's our job to prepare for it and do something about it. We must be self-reliant.

The thing about these escalators is that they are our own invention. We invent the tasks that need to be done. And most things humans do today are quite unnecessary for sustaining human life in a pure physical sense. We should never underestimate human creative invention. It's not going to be as straightforward as a factory was. It's going to be an uncomfortable, bumpy transition. Many people will be displaced, emotionally devastated, and experience deep economic hardship. That's why I am writing this. Because I know that with the right knowledge, we can ride out these bumps and find a new ride when we need to.

Which brings us back to the number one problem with school. It doesn't prepare us for life. It teaches us how to hitch a ride on a certain escalator, but it never prepares us to jump from one to another.

The hierarchy of human needs revisited

Maslow's hierarchy of needs (see figure 4.1) is frequently referred to in management texts that seek to understand human

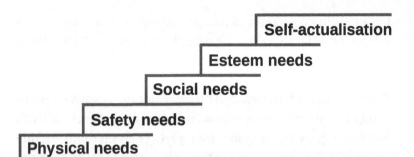

Figure 4.1: Maslow's hierarchy of needs reimagined

motivation. It also offers a useful template to shed light on the technological and social evolution of the human collective. Let's revisit the hierarchy.

Maslow contended that we must meet our most basic needs before we can move up the hierarchy to address other needs. Unless our physical needs are met, we cannot hope to satisfy higher-level needs. If we look at the hierarchy from a structural and economic point of view, we can see that the jobs people do generally follow an upward trajectory. Once our physical and safety needs are met, we focus increasingly on inventing work that is more emotionally satisfying. The easiest tasks to automate are those occupying the lower levels of the hierarchy. During the industrial era, we substituted the efforts of our own muscles and of our draft animals with machines powered by fossil fuels, which is why we still measure engines by 'horsepower'.

Senior school students were never judged on how well they could lift heavy things. The industrial age was about matching the new muscle of machines with left-brain logic. Which is why our schooling valued the classic logical subjects so highly.

Industrial theory was about using logic and machine technology to solve human problems lower down the hierarchy of our societal needs. Today we are applying the calculus of left-brain logic to the microchip. Silicon is now superseding our lower-order thinking. We don't have to memorise anything these days, and I personally think we are better off saving our mental RAM for more creative effort. When I say creative, don't think art; when I say art, don't think painting. Creativity is our ability to solve problems in new and interesting ways. Creativity is about improving outcomes by applying new methods, linking seemingly disparate elements through our personal and unique life experiences. If you are creative in any area, then in my book you're an artist. Artists invent new ideas and methods, and see things from new angles. They create new perspectives that allow us to reinvent things and achieve better outcomes. It's hard to create new value, and be seen as irreplaceable, if we merely implement and follow instructions. If we only follow rules that someone else has established, we should remember that those rules can readily be passed onto anyone they choose to replace us with, or they might as easily choose to put a machine where we once were. The more routine the task, the higher the risk. If it is merely functional, the cost-effectiveness argument will always win. But the future is still bright for less routine work.

It's time to become the artistic and creative person you were born as. It's time to find the creative spirit buried deep inside you, the one that was systematically suppressed over 12 years of schooling. Not only does the world need it, but it is quickly becoming an economic imperative. In a world where machines will blow our minds with their capabilities, the original ideas that will lift you up through the hierarchy of needs will also raise your potential economic value. The areas we were once told could never offer a living will be where the most profitable livings will take place. If there is one of you, you can bet there are thousands more who will appreciate your creative self in their ecosystem.

Many of us have postponed social, esteem and self-actualisation needs in order to meet our physical and safety needs, which are the bedrock of a civilised society. In the near future, however, the most valuable work we do will be work we want done by a human, even if a machine or robot could do it. Music, sport and entertainment provide many clues to our future. The fact that a human is creating it will be why we value it. We can listen to a recorded version of a song for free, but to see the artist perform the song live in concert offers a different kind of value; it's something that can't be substituted, and we'll pay a premium for the experience. Turning *music* from a noun into a verb changes the value for the listener dramatically. The human artistic hand and mind will command a premium in a world of physical abundance.

Ignore your weaknesses

No one is good at everything, but I believe that everyone can be exceptional, even a genius, at something. Here's a piece of advice we've been given our entire lives that is worth ignoring: 'These are your development opportunities. You need to work on these weaknesses'. You've heard this before — in a school report, an end-of-year review, from someone who happened to control some part of your short-term future. Maybe you heard it after one of your work buddies was promoted. You need to focus on this, that and the other, so you'll become a more well-rounded engineer, accountant, salesperson, chef, student. Right?

Here's the thing: that advice is for them, not you. Just think about their perspective for a moment and it all starts to make sense. A company doesn't want employees who are great at some tasks and prone to mistakes in others. They want good, well-rounded employees who are reliable if average and can turn their hand to as many things as possible with little supervision. It makes the workplace more efficient, which makes it only rational given this entire system is based on efficiency. In any case, they have to tell you something to make sense of why

Peter got that promotion. They can't just say they like him more, he looks the part or he went to the same school they did. The truth is we all have weaknesses, but some people's seem to be overlooked.

A teacher or school generally doesn't want students who excel at some things and flounder at others. They are assessed on the average aggregate performance of their classes, not on how many people discover their core competencies or their crazy natural advantage.

Strength-finding hacks

If you choose to tolerate your weaknesses, then it's worth having a clear idea of what your strengths are. Sometimes that's not as easy as it sounds, especially given that some of our core skills are not readily convertible into money. Well, that's what we were told. I used to love playing video games when I was a kid, and my mum would complain it could never lead to anything worthwhile. Yet the video game industry is expecting sales of more than US$100 billion this year, and professional video game players can now earn well over a million dollars a year by participating in e-sports where gamers play in front of live audiences. It appears that the limitations on how we earn our living are being reinvented.

If you're wondering what you want to do when you grow up (I still change my mind every few years!), here are some things to look for:

THE GRADE 3 HACK

Whatever you got in trouble for in grade 3 should form the basis of the work you do in grown-up land. Every report card I got gave me an 'excellent' rating for 'Oral Expression' while criticising me for 'too many weaknesses'. I'd point to this Oral

Expression thing and say, but hey I did well at that ... and by the way, what does it mean? The response was always the same: it means you talk too much. For many years now that strength, so evident way back in grade school, has been a significant revenue earner for me. Maybe you got in trouble for drawing in your work book; maybe you would often daydream and lose focus; maybe you got the other kids all excited about something not on the agenda; or maybe you had a talent in the playground — organising or keeping the peace? Almost certainly there was something that shone through for you, and inside that thing is the gold of what you could be doing now.

THE 10 PER CENT RULE

Every job I ever had, from flipping hamburgers to selling toilet paper (yes, I did that once), had something I really liked about it, even if the overall gig was terrible. That 10 per cent of the task we really excel at, the 10 per cent that has others in the office coming up to us for help or asking about the tricks we use to get that bit done so well. If we can find a way to do only that task, all the time, then we'll earn more and be happier for it. You may be surprised by how viable it is to turn this into a reality. Because it's a strength, you do better, gain more respect and improve to a level that others just can't compete with.

QUIT QUICKLY

To find out what works for you, try as many things as possible as quickly as possible. We do this with startups, failing our way to success by trying as many things as we can as quickly and cheaply as possible. The cool thing about doing this for work is that someone is paying you to find out what you hate doing. The quicker you quit, the quicker you can test out the next idea. Sure, stay a season, see if the seeds germinate, but don't stay much longer if the ground isn't fertile for you.

FOLLOW YOUR EFFORT

I'm passionate about lots of things I know I'm not great at. It doesn't stop me doing them, but I'm not foolish enough to take the follow-your-passion bait. Here's a better idea espoused by billionaire entrepreneur Mark Cuban: Follow your effort. Effort is a curious thing, because it tells the truth about combined talent and competence. Often it's a wonderful intersection of above-average potential with something that the market rewards. It's also worth looking back to see what we've done, to know what we ought to do.

It is often said that the best way to understand the future is to be a good historian, and this is good advice. It turns out, though, that this is a tip we can also implement in our own lives. Looking back at the footsteps we've left behind when we struggled and when we excelled may usefully inform us on what to do next.

Yes, we should try to improve. There's no doubt that we do need a portfolio of skills to navigate our world. But to focus on our weaknesses at the expense of becoming world class in areas in which we have natural talent is bordering on negligent. It's poor advice, which is very often given for the benefit of the giver, not the receiver. Working on weakness is the direct birth child of a world that has been pressuring us to conform for 200 years. If our most revered scientists and entrepreneurs had heeded this advice to work on their weaknesses instead of their gifts, we'd have been robbed of so many things we take for granted in our modern technological society. Anyone who ever achieved anything of note in this world did so through focusing on their strengths; we can always outsource our weaknesses. It's time we removed this trope from the economic game of life.

Economics is always major

As in all things, of course, there are exceptions to the rule. The one weakness we all must work on, if we have it, is economics.

IT DOESN'T MATTER WHAT YOU MAJORED IN, ECONOMICS IS <u>ALWAYS</u> MAJOR.

Economics is major because it is the one tool of trade we all share regardless of how we generate our money. If we cannot manage our money and our personal financial situation, we'll be destined for unhappiness. The basic conditions of managing our physical requirements in life always centre on money. So this is the one skill we all have to work on, *especially* if it is a weakness. And it's actually not as hard to understand as it might seem. Making the effort to understand the ins and outs of money will reduce stress in your life more than you could ever imagine. Simple rules and tools that are never taught in school, even when you study finance, are key to managing your home and family effectively. It's interesting that the word *economics* derives from the ancient Greek word *okionomia*, broadly meaning 'rules of the house' or 'household management'.

Economics is the foundation of the modern world. Not knowing how the money system really works, at both a personal and a structural level, is a bit like rolling the dice without knowing the rules of the game. No one would be crazy enough to do that. Before you play any game for the first time you ask about the rules, yet in the all-important game of life we aren't taught the money rules, and sometimes we don't even ask. The rules that matter don't emanate from accounting or finance classes, either. You don't need to know about debits or credits and where they belong in the ledger.

When it comes to money, there are basic principles and practices that never change and always work. Whether you want to get rich or just stay on top of your finances, understanding these principles will stand you in good stead for the future. The next section of this book, Part II, 'Revenue', is packed with life-changing financial hacks and insights.

Life hacks for the revolution!

1   *We become the average of the five people we spend most time with.*Your peers are important. You absorb their economics and viewpoint. Choose carefully, drop the Luddites, hang with the future focused.

2   *Develop a list of digital mentors.* Tap into the world's best thinkers in the areas you need to learn about. Organise a daily dose of intelligence and inspiration by having their wisdom delivered directly to your inbox from their blogs, podcasts, tweets and whatever they publish online. Become the average of the world's best by stealth.

3   *Ask the 10-year-old you what you would do.* This will be the best, most creative and most honest answer you'll get. At 10 you were at your entrepreneurial best. This person is still inside you. Find them.

4   *Change places.* When things aren't working, move. You are not a tree. Change where you hang out, change where you work, change where you live. Cut new ground—move. New environments present new opportunities. Leverage the core human advantage of adaptability by forcing it upon yourself.

5   *Quit.* If you don't like your work, quit as quickly as possible. Sticking it out is a mug's game, it's better to increase the sample size so you can find something you're suited to.

6   **Be self-reliant**. The biggest gift you can give yourself is the gift of self-reliance. Ask if your next move increases your independence or restricts it.

7   **Everything changes for you when** you *change*. Here's a list of things and people you can stop blaming: your negative relatives, the economy, your company, your boss, your industry, the government, politicians, your colleagues and friends. They have no influence over your success. They are the same challenges everyone faces, so focus on yourself instead.

Part II
Revenue

We are all out there rolling the dice in a real-world game of Monopoly, yet very few of us have bothered to learn how to play. Money, like most subjects, follows certain rules, and understanding these rules allows us to play the game better. Some of them can't be learned while playing the game; they're a secret that needs to be unlocked by someone who knows them and uses them. The cool thing, though, is that they are in some ways philosophical and their general principles don't change a great deal over time.

In this section we are going to investigate the truth about money in many of its forms and to discover things that never made it into the classroom. These ideas will be explored using simple, straightforward language that carefully avoids the double speak favoured by economists. I call money *revenue* because what we are interested in here are the flows of money, not just wages or investments. As soon as we think of it as revenue, we rise above the wage mentality and start to think in the way financiers do.

In the following chapters you'll learn that not all money is created equal, and that certain money is both easier to generate and less risky than we've been led to believe. And, depending on where the money is generated, the government will let you keep more of it than you might expect. There are many ways in which the system is rigged to support certain players and rules. Recognising these biases and not fearing them makes all the difference; it is in fact a core requirement for successfully negotiating the path to financial independence.

CHAPTER 5
The truth about money

I'm not sure why, but for some reason the topic of money was taboo when I was growing up. To this day many of us find it awkward to talk about how much we earn and to compare notes. Money makes people act a little strangely. Again, this starts early, and while money isn't everything, it is the glue that holds our modern lives together, so it's worth knowing how it works. People who really want to know about money have to seek out that knowledge independently. Disappointingly, it's rarely taught at school. There's some weird kind of pretence that we are actually going to school to learn, not how to earn money, but rather how to get a job. 'Don't talk about the war', but the day we leave school money becomes the battlefield of life.

The reason this stuff isn't taught in school was spelt out at the start of the book. School wasn't set up to teach you how to be rich; it was set up to teach you how to get a job in existing and emerging industries. It was set up to teach the three R's of reading, writing, and arithmetic. But money is a curious beast, and just being good at arithmetic is no guarantee of being able to manage money. And earning lots of it doesn't mean you'll understand it, or be able to keep it. That's why I'm adding the important 'R' of *Revenue*. I call it revenue on purpose, because I want people to think beyond jobs and careers to earn money and to view it objectively in its entirety, including all the possible ways money can be accumulated, and remove the wage mentality entirely. Changes in our language can literally change our lives by reframing our thinking. Knowing how revenue works, how to get it and how to make it grow, can make life easier. Get ready to learn the truth about dollars in a way that makes simple sense, and should be taught in school.

Are you being or organising?

When it comes to generating revenue we have a choice. We can either (a) be a factor of production or (b) organise the factors of production (and own them). When we are a factor of production, we are essentially a widget in a system someone else has organised. We are part of the process, playing a small role in making something happen. We are told what to do, and we are paid for our contribution to the outcome. Generally, the more important our contribution and the more irreplaceable we are, the more we are paid. The less vital or irreplaceable we are, the less we get paid.

When we organise the factors of production, we are the ones who pull together the people with the skills and assets needed to create a product or service for the market. Now our task is to imagine a product, service or event, and coordinate the factors of production (people, inputs and money) so we make more money than we spent creating it — otherwise known as a profit.

Other than in a simple trade, if you are a factor of production, then by default you will be organised by someone else for their profit. This isn't necessarily a bad thing, but it is important we understand where we are in the order of things.

Organising the factors of production is generally more profitable than *being* a factor of production (see figure 5.1). This

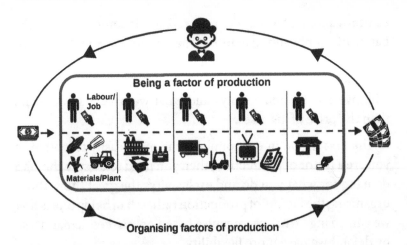

Figure 5.1: organising vs being a factor of production

is because there is usually more financial risk in the economic creation process than in the participation process. In simple terms, this is summed up in the risk-and-return maxim we so often hear about. The higher the financial risk, the higher the return should be for the person embracing that risk. People who are replaced or made redundant are always on the 'being a factor of production' side of the equation.

> **WHEN YOU ARE PART OF SOMETHING SOMEONE ELSE OWNS, YOU CAN NEVER BE IN CONTROL OF YOUR OWN FUTURE; SOMEONE ELSE IS.**

The only time you can be sure of having some control as a factor of production is when the production itself can't happen without you. For a public event such as a concert, for example, someone will devise it, organise it and sell it, but it needs the star of the show to ensure that people turn up — without *Beyoncé*, there is no concert. In this case, she will earn as much as, and most likely more than, the organiser. So it is important to pay attention to how important we are in the economic supply chain. The more skills we have, the more value we create, the more we can earn and the harder we are to replace. It comes down to the basics of supply and demand. If there is an oversupply of what we do, the price goes down and we are at risk of being replaced by another supplier or by automation. If fewer people can do what we do (limited supply) and what we have is in demand, then the price of 'us' rises.

The first lesson in economics is the most easily forgotten: if you are a factor of production, then you need to be sure there's a demand for what you do and exclusivity. The great thing about organising the factors of production rather than being one is that we can change what we organise based on market demands, so by default we have more flexibility.

Why ESTEEM matters

At the start of the book I argued that STEM (science, technology, engineering and maths) doesn't adequately cover the core educational subject areas for the new world because it ignores Economics and Entrepreneurship, leaving out 'why it matters' and 'how it fits together in the system we are all part of'. They never tell us how to bring our skills to market, to people who can benefit from them. STEM fails to recognise that organising is better than being and is a fundamental prerequisite for creating anything of value. This is why many entrepreneurs get the credit for inventions that aren't their own — I'm looking at you, Thomas Edison. Widely credited with the invention of the lightbulb, Edison was in fact just one of many contributors to the technology. What he brought along was the two missing E's of economics and entrepreneurship.

The success of any system relies on economics and entrepreneur-ship. Getting kids to focus on STEM (which of course are terrific skills the world cannot have too much of) unfortunately still reflects old-world thinking, which assigns people as widgets in the system. It's a short cut to saying, hey, learn some important stuff for our tech future, but you can leave the business side of it to 'us'. All of which is why I have proposed substituting STEM with ESTEEM.

I often wonder how many Garage Heroes — ordinary people quietly tinkering away inventively at home — there are out there who simply don't understand the business side of getting their idea up and running. Chances are you know a few such people yourself. Great gizmos with no go-to-market methodology. This is why we need these skills, and the whole community stands to benefit from getting them out there.

THE NUMBER ONE RULE FOR ALL ENTREPRENEURS IS SIMPLE: <u>ORGANISE</u> THE FACTORS OF PRODUCTION, DON'T <u>BE</u> THEM. GRADUATE FROM THE CORE SKILL YOU BRING TO THE MARKET BY BUILDING THE SYSTEMS THAT SUPPORT THE NEED FOR THAT SKILL.

Divide and conquer, economics style

We live in an increasingly complex world. We look with awe at certain technologies and industries, wondering how the heck they do it. Skyscrapers, bridges, freeway exits twisted like knots on the finger, computer equipment, energy networks, airports delivering fresh lettuce into New York City every day. Where do you even start? We can look a bit closer at the industry we work in, and admit there are so many moving parts that even though we are experts in our realm, we only know some of the bits. Wherever they sit in the hierarchy of organising or doing, no one in our modern world knows everything about how *anything* works. One of the key things that distinguishes our species is our social nature and the collective way we get things done. We divide labour to a degree unrivalled by any other animal on the planet.

In 1958 Leonard Read wrote a famous essay titled *I, Pencil*. In it he discusses the complexity involved in the creation of a simple pencil. He traces the process through the people who, working independently and interdependently, step by step transmute the raw materials into the finished product. He writes of the wood, glue, graphite, lacquer, paint, ferrule, factice, pumice and wax; and the people involved in each disparate industry, from the lighthouse keeper who guides the shipment into port to the cleaner who sweeps the factory floor. It would be fascinating to apply the same investigative unravelling to a bicycle or a smartphone, or even the takeout pizza you ordered last week.

It is true that newer technology tends to involve a level of comp-lexity that is even more difficult to understand, but as demonstrated in the *I, Pencil* essay, not understanding how things work in the world around us is not a new phenomenon. So it is vital we do not let the fear of new technology overcome the economic and social power it offers us. This revolution is kinder, more human than the last one. This time we are a few key strokes or a voice-activated search away from connecting with anyone in the world who knows about the bits we don't. We can find the people we need to organise anything. We can watch an explanatory video on demand, and most often for free. Given this gift, we should not worry about the increasing complexity. Our brain is still the most complex thing we know of in the universe, and we use it to our advantage without knowing much at all about how it does what it does. It's worth remembering this when we feel overwhelmed by the emerging technology around us. I have no idea how the mechanics of a car works, yet I've been a beneficiary of automobiles my entire life. We need only to 'drive' any technology to benefit from it, and we can usually ignore what's under the hood, leaving that part to someone else.

Since time immemorial the division of human labour has shown us that the most powerful thing we can do in life is connect. Connect people, connect assets, connect ideas, connect industries, connect geographies. I like to think of the internet as a connection revolution that happens to be underpinned by technology. The technology itself is merely the facilitator. The new connections made possible by it are where all its potential power comes from.

Think about what, in simple terms, the internet does:

» It connects cognitive surplus.

» It more efficiently allocates resources.

Cognitive surplus is the ideas and creative input of everyone connected to the internet — their content in all its forms. This surplus is almost infinite. The more than 27 billion words, in 293 languages, on Wikipedia represent the surplus wisdom of the connected crowd. You'll find a YouTube video on just about any topic, from the abstract to the absurd. There are more than 30 million cat videos alone.

Allocating resources has also been transformed. Before the internet there was simply no way of knowing what resources were available, where they could be sourced, if anyone else was using them and what the best price was. Making opaque information about assets transparent creates transactions where none previously existed. It produces new money by making what was formerly idle, active. Connecting the physical things in our world in a more open way creates efficiency and new money.

In short, if your future income involves effectively organising cognitive surplus or more efficiently allocating resources, then you will generally earn more revenue than the person next to you.

Learning to do both

School taught us how to provide cognition or to be an asset in a system; it never showed us how to organise or invent them.

Here's the thing: there's no rule saying you can't do both at the same time. We can be a widget earning income while we are learning to build our own system of production. In fact, there is no better way to learn than from the inside. Even if your work is kind of terrible, you'll see clearly how *not* to do things, and observing the mistakes on display around you is one of the best ways of learning how to do anything well. Anyone can start to learn the art of entrepreneurship on the side, at night, on the weekend or while earning a living in a conventional way. You just need to start. Keep your costs low and have a crack. More on this in Part III, 'Reinvention'.

It's mostly about being curious and courageous. Know that you don't know it all, and do it anyway. Learning as you go along by making commonsense decisions and asking the people who do know will take you much further than you'd believe. Unless you're silly enough to sink all your assets into a single venture, or endanger someone else's livelihood, the risk of having a crack is almost non-existent. No one is going to starve to death, go homeless or get eaten by a tiger. The fear of starting something entrepreneurial is mostly in our heads, rooted in our childhood indoctrination about not making mistakes, not takings risks, avoiding any red pen next to our names. The worst-case scenario is we get better at what we already do and make new connections we can leverage the next time we try. In any case, failure is not the opposite of success; inaction is. While we are 'failing' we are *progressively realising* our worthy ideal.

In his 2016 film documentary *HyperNormalisation*, Adam Curtis suggests one explanation for why there seem to be so many astounding political and social paradoxes in our time.

There has never been a period of such technological revolution or such access to global resources, yet there is increasing wealth disparity and growing fear for the future. His contention is that, if a system is broken — and we know it is broken if there seems to be no valid alternative — we carry on as if everything was okay and pretend to ourselves that the status quo is acceptable. The title of the film is taken from an interesting book by Alexei Yurchak, who used it to describe the Soviet Union in the late 1980s, just before it collapsed.

'Back then,' Curtis has explained in an interview, 'everyone knew that the system was fake ... that the politicians had absolutely no control over the economy .... and because there was no alternative everyone regarded it as normal, and he [Yurchak] coined this phrase *HyperNormalisation*. Meaning that the fakeness was just accepted because it was normal'.

Curtis describes the kind of economic inaction and political inertia we suffer from when we don't have a real plan of what we can do instead. Politicians tell you stories of how they'll change the world for you and improve your economic circumstances, when in reality their promises are mostly hollow. But if you follow the reinvention opportunities presented in the final part of this book, you'll know exactly what to do. You'll see there is an alternative, but one that is in your interest and circumvents traditional power structures. Maybe that's why this information is not broadcast widely — it is something of an underground movement — and instead you must seek it out.

The jobs and growth hoax

When it comes to inaction, there is no more pernicious promise made by politicians than the one of jobs and growth. It sends all the wrong messages to society. It's another way of saying, don't worry we've got it covered. It's an almost nostalgic promise of a return to mythical boom times, when life was easier and the economy sailed along smoothly. It appeals to our yearning for a simple past that was somehow better, when politicians were principled and noble, and growth was steady and organic.

The real problem is how this mindset makes people think. It entrenches a belief that someone else will make it happen for us. They'll fix the problems each of us is facing. They'll fix our industry, they'll make sure our offering is in demand and we'll all have more money and opportunity than we had before, because 'growth' will make it so. If we'd just vote them in, everything will be okay. The politician promises jobs for hard-working people, and the hard-working people respond, 'You're gonna create jobs? That's fantastic, just what we need. We'll be waiting over here for when those jobs are created. Let us know, give us a hoy as soon as they arrive, and we promise to come running and give you all our effort with the skills we've already got. Thanks for doing this, it really does make life a bit easier, and now I can stop worrying. I'd much prefer just to keep doing the work I've always done. Keep me updated. I'll be just over here'.

Here's the thing: this thinking is inside out. It's telling people to wait for someone to serve them, that the system will deliver people's needs and that they just need a little faith and patience. It deprives people of initiative and self-reliance. It teaches us to be receivers, not creators. It subconsciously trains people to think about participating only as labour, rather than as someone who generates revenue from whatever source they may have created from the resources they have. It ignores the reality that many people will need to reinvent themselves so they have something the changing market demands. It discourages the idea of creating something from nothing to generate your own independent revenue stream, whether as a freelancer or through a new business startup. Subtly, it creates a passive society rather than one that actively seeks and invents economic opportunity through solving people's problems in exchange for money. That's why I don't like using the word jobs; it's just too passive. I much prefer revenue.

REVENUE TELLS ME THERE ARE MANY WAYS TO GENERATE IT; JOBS, ON THE OTHER HAND, SUGGESTS MONEY CAN ONLY COME FROM THAT SINGLE SOURCE, AND IT'S JUST NOT TRUE. IT LIMITS PEOPLE'S THINKING, AND THEREFORE LIMITS WHAT SOCIETY CREATES.

We deserve more than this from government; we deserve the respect that goes with the truth of what the world needs and how we ought to respond to this need. We are treated like economic outpatients, like children unable to cope with the truth about economic changes to the landscape.

While many of the old, well-paid manufacturing-era jobs are simply not coming back, new opportunities are constantly emerging. The market doesn't care what politicians promise, what skills you've got today or that growth was stronger at some time way back when. The market delivers what people demand and prices it based on scarcity. The reason that Facebook has such a giant market capitalisation (the valuation of the company) is because it has attracted the attention of 2.4 billion people, and attention is one of the scarcest commodities in today's market, where:

DEMAND × SCARCITY = VALUE THE MARKET PUTS ON SOMETHING.

In lay terms we must constantly ask ourselves this about any form of economic activity we are involved in: *How much do people want it, and how much of it is out there?*

Life changes when we change. Life gets better when we get better. We ought to stop wishing things were easier and start ensuring we have more to offer. The best, least stressful course we can take is to invest in ourselves. Until we do that, how can we expect anyone else, or the market, to invest in us? Skills used to be something we acquired. Now they are something we must continually curate. Just as we must regularly upgrade the software on our devices, we must upgrade the software of our grey matter by uploading new information and skills the market values. When we do, the upside is enormous.

CHAPTER 6
Money isn't money

What is money? It's hard to define it in a way that makes sense to all of us, rather than just to economists. Historically it has taken many forms too, from shark's teeth and cowry shells, to physical commodities and grain receipts, to cheques, coins and paper money, to debt and cryptography. In fact, most money in the world doesn't even exist. Less than 10 per cent of the money people own or can make claim to actually exists in a physical form as little pieces of paper or metal discs with important people's heads on them. Most money these days is just a number stored electronically somewhere against which someone can claim at some future point in time. The fact is the stability of the entire modern monetary system relies on people not all wanting it back on the same day.

Delivering against a future promise

In many ways money is a kind of myth based on implied power structures and hierarchies. Which brings us back to the question of a definition of money, a definition that is not about 'currency' as we know it, a definition that creates meaning and remains true regardless of the currency of the day. I'm also not talking about the elements that make a currency functional (acceptance, medium of exchange, divisibility or stored value). Rather, I'm talking about what it means to people in a human sense. So here it is:

MONEY REPRESENTS THE VALUE AND SECURITY OF A FUTURE PROMISE.

That's all money is. Sure, we set different prices on different promises, but the value is based on these future expectations — promises people and organisations make each other and the expectation that the exchange will deliver against that promise. When the promise is broken by one party, the money disappears. It might happen immediately or later, but if the promise is not fulfilled, the trust is broken and the parties can't transact in future, because this promise equates to the deepest human social contract. I'm not trying to invent some fancy, super-nuanced definition of money. I'm suggesting that once we view money like this, it frees up our mind to understand why some people seem to attract more money than others. We can free ourselves from the numbers and start thinking about it in terms of value creation. We can start thinking about what causes it to move in the patterns it does, and about trust and expectations, which are essential before any money changes hands. So let's look at this in practical terms, focusing on the types of monetary exchanges we've all made in the past:

» *Buying a chocolate bar.* We exchange a small sum of money for a micro-pleasure. Little trust is required because the price is small and the time gap between purchase and delivery is short.

» *Buying groceries.* Prices are still small, and we can shift our trust quickly if the product delivery doesn't keep the product performance promise.

» *Buying insurance.* The price is quite high and we put a lot of trust in the insurer to pay up if needed. The insurer reduces its risk by assessing our wider profile as an economic risk.

» *Buying a house.* The price is so high, and the risk so great, that the government needs to get involved in the transfer. Large sums of money are loaned on the basis of our potential ability to make future payments, which is based on the probability of our maintaining our income. The bank's risk is so high that it can seize the house if the trust is broken. Both parties believe in the future promise that the house price will rise. Problems arise when this doesn't happen.

» *Getting a job.* A company promises to give us money based on the service we promise to deliver and the complexity of the work to be done. The exchange is prolonged and ongoing, requiring paper trails to show that each party can deliver the promised value to the other. Minimum-wage workers are highly replaceable with little risk to the employer, so the formalities of the transaction are much reduced.

» *Investing in shares.* A company promises to deliver a return on shareholder investment. The value of a share is higher when the price to buy it is greater relative to the amount the company earns per share (the price/earnings ratio).[11] This reflects the level of trust that the company will keep its earnings promise. The greater this trust, the stronger (the more 'blue chip') the company for investors.

» *Loaning money to a friend.* This form of social contract is based on friendship. The cost of not keeping a promise to repay the lender is to lose a friend. When we have such social trust, no direct exchange of products or services is involved.

» *Spending on a credit card.* The bank knows future repayment is 'unsecured' (whereas on a house it is secured by a mortgage). The bank mitigates this lower trust by making the interest rate exorbitant to reflect this future promise risk.

» *Visiting a doctor.* Doctors are among the most trusted service providers. We know they've done years of government-vetted study. Our belief that they will deliver on the promise of improved health is so great that we pay for something without even knowing what it is or how it works. Pure trust.

Our role, economically at least, is to increase the future value of our promise, first in perception terms and eventually in actual delivery. The stronger our brand (our promise), the more trusted we are. When the trust is higher, sometimes we can command a premium for our promise, a premium that is often disproportionate to the relative value of delivery. Sometimes we'll garner the trust of others to leverage down the line — formal education is one of these routes. While there is no guarantee that someone formally trained in a certain skill will be better than the self-taught person, the promise from the external party provides weight. Trust is one of our most powerful emotions.

There's a reason we need to be able to conceptualise money in this way. It helps us cross the chasm. Once your mindset is altered — and believe me, once you start thinking of money in this way, there is no going back — then you have a higher chance of trusting yourself, and this is the first thing you need to be able to do before you can enter the realm of freelance work and entrepreneurship, because intuitively you know you are trustworthy. You keep your promises.

The three types of money

Because money is not real but is a future promise, there are different types of money. Different types of promises and values are set against delivery of those promises. In some ways money is a bit like transport. Different types of money move at different speeds, some modes of monetary transport are more efficient than others, and different types of money generate different returns on effort. Yes, you read that right. Certain types of money have a higher return on effort. Not all money is created equal. There are three types of money: *earned money, invested money* and *invented money*.

1. EARNED MONEY (WAGES OR SALARY – HIGH PROBABILITY – LOW RETURN)

We receive a payment for work undertaken for someone else. This someone else could be a person, a corporation or a government. This is the type of money that most of the world lives on. We get paid for the labour we provide. There is a direct link between the work done and the money received. The more skilled the labour, the higher it is paid. Generally, this type of money has the lowest return on effort and the highest probability. That is because we are choosing to be a factor of production. We get paid per hour for the work we do, but the hourly rate is based on the amount of value we create and the scarcity of what we provide. Minimum-wage workers don't just get $X an hour; they create $X of value for each hour they are there. We can increase the amount we earn per hour, but this upside is restricted because we can never squeeze more hours into the day. This is active earning. We only ever earn this money when we are 'present' — school taught us how to do this — and the 'smart kids' got into the course that earned more per hour. It's ironic that we had to say 'present' when the roll was called every morning in the classroom.

2. INVESTED MONEY (EQUITY AND PROPERTY – MEDIUM PROBABILITY – MEDIUM RETURN AND RISK)

This is passive earning. We place our excess money into a business or a property in order to generate a return. Equity refers to having a share in any kind of business, big or small, public or private. Property refers to putting money into buildings or plant and equipment. The return can be in dividends or rents. We are paid an amount by the people who use our money or the business we invest in, or we get rent back from the property we let others use. We can also get a return from selling the shares or property for a higher price than we paid for them, which is called *capital gains*, so we end up with more money than we put in. An asset like this usually goes up in value when the returns go up or more people think the return will increase at some point in the future. This is the type of money you can earn while you sleep. You don't have to do the work; you put your money in the asset itself (the business or property), which is why we hear the expression 'let your money work for you'.

The risk of trying to create *invested money* covers a wide spectrum. Very safe investments include bank interest and government bonds. Medium-risk investments include residential property and blue-chip shares (in Apple Computer, for instance). They can also include speculative investments such as mining shares or futures, development projects or plantations. The higher the risk, the higher the return you'd expect. You don't have to be constantly present to get this money, but to do it right requires that the investment be given a level of attention and 'presence'. It's also done best when the investor understands the flow of 'promises' and the probability they will be kept by the parties in that supply chain.

3. INVENTED MONEY (ENTREPRENEURSHIP – HIGHEST RISK – HIGHEST RETURN)

This is what entrepreneurs do. They imagine a new way to put resources together, to solve people's problems for a monetary reward that is greater than their costs in pulling the resources together. The margin (the sum of money after all costs have been taken into account) is the profit. An entrepreneur who makes a profit literally invents money. This is because at the end of the process there is more money than there was at the start. Economists call it the multiplier effect. The resources used could include people, property, plant, raw materials, technology, other people's money — anything. When a system is built around entrepreneurial activities that can consistently deliver these results, then a 'business' is created. Property 'development' is an example of this process.

This type of money sits at the top of the hierarchy of the three types of money because it makes most of the earned and invested money possible and has the highest return on effort. It is seen as being the most risky, given that the monetary return may not kick in until far in the future, or the venture may not succeed at all. It is also true that historically the cost of acquiring the resources needed to 'invent money' was prohibitive. In the industrial age the barriers to entry were typically too high for most people to compete with an established firm, especially within traditional industrial sectors such as manufacturing. But in the past 20 years the barriers to entry for entrepreneurs have fallen to historic lows. It has never been easier to start a new venture.

From ownership to access

Starting a venture has generally been seen as risky because the resources *required* had to be *acquired*. Without the money, there could be no inputs, and without the needed inputs there was no venture. Conversely, now we've entered the age of the virtual venture, where anyone can organise the factors of production without taking ownership, a venture in a sense 'virtualises' profit. What we once had to own, we can now simply access. While this is clearly happening on the consumer side of the ledger, it's also true for business ventures. We can get funding from future customers through crowdfunding, we can use a factory we don't own, we can utilise people who aren't employees, we can sell on other people's platforms, we can promote on channels we didn't pay for. We can even get the idea online or find a co-founder on a startup dating website. The traditional process of generating money, largely restricted to an 'elite' class, has been democratised to allow new, much lower levels of entry. This time it *is* different. There has never been a better time to invent money.

Figure 6.1 illustrates the risks/benefits and probabilities for the three types of money and is designed to represent an ideology, a way of thinking about different types of money.

In a capitalist economy there are no rules to stop anyone, whatever their education or background, from changing the type of money they accumulate. We can all learn how to do it. But there is one irrefutable truth about money, which is evidenced by the three types of money.

INVESTED MONEY AND INVENTED MONEY ARE BETTER THAN EARNED MONEY FOR ONE SIMPLE REASON: PROFITS ARE BETTER THAN WAGES.

This is true for reasons that go beyond the fact that you literally 'invent money'. The first is that once you have built a system that makes profits, you can sell that enterprise to someone else. And when you do, you'll be selling it for more than how much money it makes each party immediately; you'll

(A)

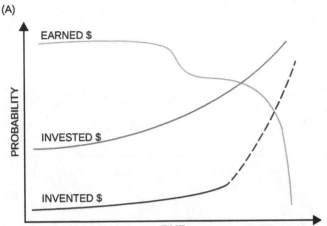

The probability of earned money is higher. There's often a dip in the later career redundancy phase, but an inevitability of permanent decline with age and changes in demand of certain skills. You'll also notice invented money has the lowest probability, but it can increase rapidly for those who keep at it. The dotted line represents the long possibility of success.

(B)

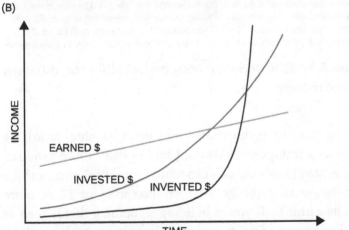

Earned money for most people grows at a steady small percentage for most of their career. Invested money has steady growth, and if reinvested compounds to higher and higher returns over time. Invented money depends on success—when it happens it results in exponential 'return of effort'. It often takes many tries before it happens, and most people give up too early.

Figure 6.1: risks/benefits and probabilities of different types of money *(Continued)*

(C)

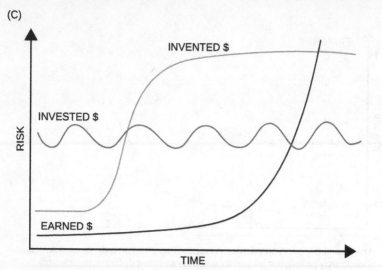

Earning money is very low risk for most of our lives. But as we age, we often get replaced by cheaper workers, machines and, shortly, artificial intelligence— the lucky ones get to retire, but earned money still ends up at zero. Invested money is always a bumpy ride, but mid-range risk. Invented money is very low risk in early adult life: we have nothing to lose and everything to gain. As our income and our opportunity cost increase the risk becomes high for most people. The art is then working out a low-cost way to learn how to invent money.

Figure 6.1: risks/benefits and probabilities of different types of money

factor in many years of earnings (the price/earnings ratio). It's the future earnings others would buy — that 'future promise' again. A small business can expect to be sold for two or three times its annual earnings, a larger enterprise for 10 or more times its earnings. If you're building something that is seen as a significant part of the future economy, the multiple at which you assess those future profits can be astounding. What this means is that for every dollar you earn in profit, or 'invent', you receive many more dollars. Every dollar invented potentially becomes two, three or even 10 dollars if you decide to sell the profit-making system. You can never sell your job.

Again, I must have been off sick the day they taught this in school.

Wages, profits and tax

Once we can overcome the risks that go with investing and inventing money, they are better than earning money in every way. They are easier to generate. They tend to grow. They can be reinvested, and there is no limit to how much of them you can accumulate. Earned wages happen at a maximum of 24 hours each day. When you are organising for profit, you are gaining part of other people's 24 hours.

Another reason they are better relates to how the economic system treats them. Strangely, while profits are better and, once a business is established, easier to get, they are taxed at a lower rate than wages. What a great reminder that he who holds the gold makes the rules! It is strange indeed, but in most countries a corporation will pay a lower tax rate than the top marginal tax rate for earned money. In Australia, where I live, the top marginal rate for earned money is currently 45 cents in every dollar. However, the company tax rate in Australia is between 28 cents and 30 cents in every dollar, depending on the size of the enterprise. Politicians and the government will point out that once profits are received by an individual through a company their earnings revert back to their personal tax rate. However, these profits can be retained, reinvested and distributed in other ways, maintaining the tax advantage, which is also a trick to keep the outsiders at ease.

It sounds unfair that a company can pay less tax than a person, particularly when a company is simply meant to represent a group of people (*corporation* comes from Latin and means 'body of people'). The structure of companies was originally shaped to limit the personal liability of individuals taking collective financial risk, which ought to benefit consumer society. The taxation pattern is the same in most developed nations. I personally think it is immoral, but while they apply we should use the rules to our and our family's advantage. Even a single-person freelancer can take advantage of a company tax structure. It's another simple reason why moving beyond the wage economy has dramatic benefits. Just changing where your money is paid — to a company you own and control rather than to you personally — can result in a 15 per cent take-home pay rise. Add to this the reasons profits are better than wages: the allowable deductions a company can claim before profit are significantly advantageous in comparison to an individual's deductibles.

The justification for these lower tax rates for corporations is a bit of a trick too. It's linked to trickle-down economics theory,[12] which claims that lower tax rates for companies will encourage investment, which will create economic growth from which wage earners and society will benefit. The fundamental problem with this argument is that all money is part of a cycle. I like to think of it as a circle that can grow (or shrink) with each cycle. We could as easily argue that wage earners with lower tax rates would have more to spend, which would increase demand for goods and services, generating further demand for investment in consumer products. The argument is a hoax introduced for the rich by the rich. It's stuff like this that subsidises the 1 per cent elite. The reason most of us aren't aware of these truths is that we never got the lessons in economics we so desperately needed.

The tax rates on profits through companies isn't where it ends either. Profits from invested money also receive a massive tax bonus in Australia. Any profit you receive from capital gains through 'invested money' (selling shares at a price higher than you paid, or selling a property or company for a profit) is taxed at half the investor's tax rate on their earned money. This is a core reason behind the move by large corporations to reward their executives with equity payments. It's no wonder the rich get richer. Not only do they generally have more excess money to invest, but when they do so and make a profit, they get an advantage earned money doesn't get. This is why we must move to generate money through investments. Not only can this money be earned while we sleep, but the tax advantages are incredible: the most anyone ever pays for tax on capital gains in Australia is 22.5 per cent on the profit. Work hard and earn well above average wages and you could be rewarded by an unintended joint venture with the government, who'll take 45 per cent of every dollar you generate. I have criticised this tax disparity between companies and people, describing it as immoral. It shouldn't exist, but given that it does, it's incumbent on us to take advantage of it — and share the knowledge of what is possible for individuals as well. We ought to restructure our revenue streams. Only when we remove this asymmetry of how we earn and structure money can the playing field be levelled and a fairer society be created. The wider knowledge of possibilities and truth changes everything.

CHAPTER 7
The seeds of greatness

Money can't really be used for that many things. We can certainly buy countless items with it, but from a category viewpoint there are only a few things we can do with money. Once we understand these categories it really becomes quite simple to accumulate more money and make your life simpler, financially at least.

We start off with two choices once money arrives, say as a number in a computer somewhere: we can either spend it or save it. That's it, the only two options. And here's where I have to drop a couple of truth bombs. It may sound like cultural heresy, but there is an infallible, historical truth about money: the ability to save is key to everything. I'm not saying you have to be a miser, but unless you can save a portion of what you earn, you'll never become self-reliant or live an independent life. It doesn't matter what 'type' of money you earn; unless you keep some for yourself, everything else becomes futile. There are many ways to phrase this truth, and it is useful to cover a few maxims relating to it, to provide both a context and a quantum to how much it really matters.

Spent money vs invested money

American entrepreneur and billionaire W. Clement Stone built his fortune in insurance and publishing, but he was a strong believer in basic financial principles. He once said, 'If you cannot save, then the seeds of greatness are not within you'.

Wow, what a powerful statement. What I love about it is its accessibility. He didn't say how much you have to save, or how much you have to earn, just that you need to be able to set aside an amount of it. Even someone on minimum wage can save 1 per cent of what they earn. It is the most basic financial challenge to prove to ourselves we have the capacity to think ahead and delay gratification in a small way. If we can't exercise enough self-control to save, then it would be a waste of our time to even try to start a business. It's really just an attitude; even a small percentage of a modest income is enough to provide direction and momentum. Anyone who has saved money understands the pride and self-esteem that come with it. You can start to believe in the upside of your decisions.

I was once told a simple life hack that's so obvious yet I'd never thought of it: 'Save half your money, and only work every second year.'

Think about it. If we could save half our income, we'd be able to take every second year off work! We could go and pursue something else, learn something new, explore. That's the power of savings right there, articulated in a different way. Saving creates options. I'm not saying you'd want to or even could do that, because you'd be back at ground zero every two years, but it opens the mind to the power of savings.

Remember, you 'get paid' for savings because they become money type number two: invested money. Spent money is dead money — it disappears. Even worse, often the things we buy need to be maintained and serviced, so they cost money to own, not just to buy. Cars, clothes, phones, computers, houses, almost everything we spend money on, require us to spend more money just to keep them alive. They need to be kept functional, cleaned, insured, topped up, updated, enhanced, furnished, stored, secured. They are not isolated, one-off expenses but carefully designed money drains that feed the industries that produce them. It's always worth appraising the maintenance cost of anything we buy, and, as you can imagine, it's rarely in the interest of the seller to tell you what those costs are likely to be. It's why they invented small print.

This leads us to the number one financial problem people, in developed economies at least, face today. The root of it is not that they have credit card debt, or that they can't afford the rent or the car repayments. It's simply that they spend money they should have saved. When they have a choice to spend or to save that dollar, they spend more than they have. Today greedy financial institutions make it far too easy for us to buy on credit. If you can't afford it, don't buy it. If I don't have the money in cash or equivalent to buy something I want, I will not buy it. Yes, it takes discipline, but I'd rather carry the small weight of frequent and valuable disciplines than break my back later under a tonne of debt.

**FORMULA FOR MISERY: SPEND MORE THAN YOU EARN.
FORMULA FOR HAPPINESS: SPEND LESS THAN YOU EARN.**

A person earning $2000 a week and spending $2200 will always be poorer than a person earning $1000 a week and saving $200 of it. The $200 either side of the earnings equation makes all the difference. It's not just a financial thing either; it soothes the soul of the saver.

Where did it go? The necessities confusion

Okay, so we need to be a bit human with all this savings stuff. Saving is totally vital to success, but life is to be enjoyed. As I said, it's not about saving every cent, it's about that habit. Using your earnings to buy stuff is incredibly enjoyable. Travelling, eating out, shopping for clothes, toys and technology, especially when rewarding work done, are among the great pleasures in life. But we must always remember that if we spend more than we earn, we'll always be a widget in someone else's production.

You've probably read in the mainstream press that the cost of living is surging and it's never been harder to make ends meet. The truth is, as I argued in my first book, *The Great Fragmentation*, a bigger lie has never been told. It's hard to think of things that are more expensive now than they were 10, 20 or 50 years ago. Here's a fact that should bust this cost-of-living conspiracy wide open: among the items we all buy are groceries, television, family car, clothes, phones, data, computers, hotels, flights and food ... and they've *all* become much cheaper to buy. The simplest confirmation of the truth about prices is this: the CPI has been lower than the wages growth index on average since 1946 in Australia. The cost of living relative to what we earn has gone down. What hasn't declined is our insatiable appetite to consume.

Part of the problem is the consumer culture mind trap. Luxuries are passed off as modern-day necessities. Streaming pixels on retina screens of shiny, life-enhancing potential. Handheld devices crying like babies for redundant updates. A virtual community of ultra-consumers, carving out a path to the supposed life worth living. The Kardashians show us what this looks like, and we mere humans mistake these accessories for essentials. We need to remember that most of what we see in the media and advertising is a façade that has little to do with happiness.

While we seem to be constantly assailed by novel ways to divest our funds for the useless, it seems the problem isn't new. Eighteenth-century French political philosopher Charles de Montesquieu wrote:

If we only wanted to be happy, it would be easy; but we want to be happier than other people, and that is almost always difficult, since we think them happier than they are.

My bet is that the Kardashians are miserable.

Most of us tend to remember growing up with less than our kids have, or at least our parents tell us how much more we have than they did. This is not some kind of parental chicanery to make us appreciate life a little more. It's mostly true. When we were discussing current standards of living, my father asked me a few questions that helped remind me how much we now spend on the nice rather than the necessary.

'When you were a kid, how many times did we go out for breakfast?'

'*None.*'

'How many times did we stay in fancy hotels for a holiday?'

'*None.*'

'How many times did you catch an aeroplane before you were 18?'

'*Once.*'

'How many pairs of shoes did you have?'

'*Two — school and runners.*'

'How many televisions did we have?'

'*One.*'

'Did you have your own bedroom?'

'No, I shared it with my brother until I was 18.'

'When did you get your first phone?'

'When I left home.'

'Where did most of your clothes come from?'

'My older brother.'

'How many paid lessons [swimming, musical instruments, languages] did you have?'

'One. I was learning to play drums.'

'How many birthday parties at a catered party venue did you go to?'

'None. Parties used to be in the backyard with a homemade cake, pin-the-tail-on-the-donkey and musical chairs.'

'How old were you when we got lucky enough to buy brand-name goods and clothes?'

'Well into my teens.'

'How many families had big SUV cars?'

'None. We all squeezed into sedans.'

'Where did you get your hair cut?'

'At home. Mum used kitchen scissors.'

And you know what? The times I look back on with the greatest fondness are those when we made do with what we had. They taught me both how to be happier with less, and how to appreciate the upside I've been lucky enough to achieve.

We spend so much of our income on the nice-to-haves that we've confused them with necessities. They are the new normal, and humans are great comparison machines. I'm not going to list the nonessentials, but we know what they are deep in our heart. We also know we could find a way to save at least a little of our income to start on the trajectory towards a surplus.

When I left the corporate sector for the first time to do my own startups, I had to make some hard decisions on going without certain comforts. I had a very nice car, but I decided to sell it and catch public transport instead. Yes, it took me two hours to get to meetings that would have taken half an hour in the car, but I was driven by the truth of doing what was necessary to achieve what was possible. I used the down time to prepare and read and learn. I turned it into a positive experience. I moved back into my old bedroom at home to save cash I could put into business so I wouldn't get dragged back into the corporate vortex. There were more of these examples, but you get the picture. I'm not saying you need to go back and live with your parents, but when we honestly assess our expenditures we'll find we can do without many things that are nice to have, at least temporarily, to get in front with our savings ratio. The ratio that gives us a chance to try something else — the freedom fund.

IF YOU CAN'T AGREE WITH WHAT I'VE SAID HERE ABOUT SAVING, THEN YOU SHOULD PUT THIS BOOK DOWN AND NOT INVEST ANY MORE TIME IN READING IT. BECAUSE I CAN'T HELP YOU FROM HERE. IF YOU DO NOT UNDERSTAND OR BELIEVE IN THIS TRUTH, THEN YOU WON'T BE ABLE TO IMPLEMENT THE ADVICE THAT FOLLOWS.

Society says spend

It's not just the perception of perfect lives conveyed in public social forums that influences us to consume. It's part of the fabric that holds modern society together. Just think about the incentives of society's most powerful institutions. Our government collects funds through taxes, which are generally based on consumption. They get a clip when we buy anything. They get 30 per cent of the profit any company makes selling stuff to us. Income tax is collected mainly from people working for companies, who employ people only when they sell enough stuff. Corporations survive only when we spend. Even our financial institutions, the one set of corporations who are meant to be on our side, financially at least, do better when we put money down on the plastic magic carpet credit card or get a loan. They make money when we spend money we don't have. It's no wonder we don't hear much about the comparative advantages of saving rather than spending our money.

Saving doesn't make anyone rich but you. This is why almost every advertisement you've ever seen provides advice on spending. The government and our corporations have no incentive to teach people the importance of saving. The more people spend, the more 'jobs' and taxpayers there are, and the less pressure there is on social services. I've seen lots of government service announcements on things we should be doing, never one that tells us the importance of saving our money. But I know they know that saving is important, because every other advertisement they run is telling us what to do so we save *them* money, discouraging behaviours that are expensive to society — driving safety and health messages, for example. I can't remember ever getting a lesson on what to do with money in school and, given the above, it's not surprising. So it's up to us to teach each other, our kids and our friends — we owe each other that much.

So next time, before you spend money on something you know you can't afford, ask yourself if you'd rather a temporary pleasure and comfort now, or the opportunity for infinite comfort later. Our ability to delay gratification is a core human principle, both psychologically and financially. It is true for study, work, eating, exercise and everything that affects our wellbeing: the ability to endure short-term pain or deprivation is what puts us ahead of the pack. If this isn't quite motivating enough, then we can always remember the sage advice of Tyler Durden, lead character in the movie *Fight Club*: 'The things you own end up owing you'.

Finance is a game

I'm very aware of the contradiction in all this. On the one hand I'm talking up the benefits of saving, while on the other I'm saying that 'inventing money' through organising factors of production will lift you to the top of the financial hierarchy. The need to save is the opposite of what I'm encouraging you to create (people's need to spend, so you can profit from their spending). I get it, it is kind of strange and paradoxical. But it is in some ways a game. Finance is a game we are all playing, and we really don't have a choice. The only way we can stop playing is if we go find ourselves a place under a banana tree somewhere and live off the land.

Living in a modern, civilised, technological society means there will be winners and losers in all this. And it is not as if we have to convince people to go out there and spend; there's enough of that happening without any extra encouragement needed. In any case, the way we make money (more on this in Part III, 'Reinvention') can have a very positive impact on other people's lives, if we create something better or more efficient, providing greater benefits than what it replaces, so it isn't all bad anyway. The crux of it is this: some will do better than others. You're making the effort to read this book, and I'm trying to share a winning formula with those who care enough about their future that they'll invest time in improving it.

The three places money can be stored

Non-consumption money, like tangible things, needs to be stored somewhere. Sounds weird, right? But as with grain or milk, where we put it has an impact on its shelf life. Like food, it can go bad. Like water, it can evaporate or accumulate. Where we put it is what makes all the difference. Now we know we have the choice to either spend or save, and we've agreed that we need to save a portion of the money, or should I say revenue, we generate, where can we put it?

When we say 'stored', we are talking about where we allocate our savings. And it turns out there are only three places that money can be stored. It can only ever be stored as *cash, property* or *equity*.

1. CASH

This is the money we keep in our purse, wallet, pocket or backpack, under the bed, in the freezer (don't do this; criminals always look here), or as cash deposits in bank accounts. It is money we keep ready to use. It's transactional in nature, on hand when we need it, say for unexpected emergencies. It shouldn't be a place for permanent storage or for storage of large sums of money. The reason is that money stored in this way goes down in value. It does this in a couple of ways. The first is that it is far easier to spend money which is readily available. Stored here it can steal from our savings and increase our consumption.

But the more important factor is that a dollar tomorrow is worth less than a dollar today. A dollar that we don't put into the market doesn't get a return. It's worth less, because a dollar that is put into the market, where it generates dividends and rents, comes to be worth the original dollar plus whatever it earns. Accountants call this the *time value of money*. If the money itself is not invested where it can get a return on investment, its value declines compared with money that is active in the market. It's the difference between active and inactive capital. It's a bit like our body: the less we use it, the less power it has to generate something on our behalf. We should keep only small amounts of our available money in this place — money for security and transactions — because it is the least effective place to keep it.

OUR GOAL SHOULD BE TO PUT EXCESS MONEY TO WORK AND USE IT TO GENERATE MORE 'INVESTED MONEY' OR TOWARDS ENTREPRENEURIAL ACTIVITIES THAT 'INVENT MONEY'.

2. PROPERTY

This is money we put into real estate — land, houses, apartments, buildings, factories, warehouses and offices. We can choose to live in them, rent them out to other people to live in or rent them out to businesses.

These are good places to store money because they most often generate a return on the money invested. Furthermore, unlike cash, the value of the dollar we put here is usually worth more the next year. This happens in two ways. First, we get rent for the use of that property, or we reduce our own cost of living by reducing our need to pay rent to live somewhere else. The rent puts money into our hands simply because we control the property asset. Interestingly, we don't necessarily have to own the property to extract rent; we just need to control the asset. Second, when we own the asset, we also gain money as it appreciates in value. If it is worth 10 per cent more next year, the original money we put into it will then be worth 10 per cent more. We can sell it at a profit, and keep the money we made from rent. Because the money was 'invested money', it continues to grow in value.

This has been the greatest source of wealth creation since the dawn of time. Land, by definition, is scarce, has a limited supply and, when chosen well, can generate above-average returns on investment. But the real reason property generates more wealth than other sources is that it is viewed as more secure. Of course there are exceptions to this — mortgage-backed securities during the GFC come to mind — but because property is seen as secure, and when it is backed by rents and leases, financial institutions will lend money to acquire it.

In this case, if you have only 10 per cent of the funds to buy some real estate, and you borrow 90 per cent of its value, and it goes up by 10 per cent in a year, then in real terms you've doubled your money through borrowing other people's money. This is why property has such a success rate in generating wealth over time. Of course a property's value can drop, and for this reason it should be viewed as a place to store money for the medium to long term. Getting in and out of property is time consuming and costly, which is restrictive but also part of the reason for its stability. It also should not be undertaken unless the return is reasonable, and it is likely to be in demand by others if the renter (people or corporation) leave town.

Historically, over the long term property goes up in value. It also requires a far lower skill base than most other investments. Dumb money can do very well; often all the investor needs to be able to do is 'hang on' long enough. Simple economics of supply and demand drive this, but even taking into account wages growth over time (2 to 3 per cent per annum in Australia for the past 60 years), we can see that people have more money to compete for property purchases every year.

3. EQUITY

Equity is money we put into a business of any kind. It could be a business we own and operate, a business someone else owns and operates, a tiny mum-and-dad business, a giant enterprise ... or anything in between. It could be a private company or a public company traded on the stock exchange. It includes money put into an investment fund, superannuation or a 401k, stocks we buy ourselves on the share market, a small business we buy, a partnership we form or even money we put into a startup business. It could involve investing in a business that is well established or bearing the risk to get something new started.

This is also a good place to put money, because we get a return in the form of dividends. In short, this is putting money into organising the factors of production for a profit. Putting money into equity works in a similar way to putting it into property. Instead of rent, we get dividends — our share of the profits the company made through 'inventing money'. It's just a different type of investment. As with property, we hope for regular returns, and for the value of the thing we invested in to rise.

Equity investments have a few important differences, though. The dividends tend to be less frequent than rent — generally quarterly, bi-annually or annually, rather than weekly or monthly. Equity investments also tend to be higher risk, with greater fluctuations in financial performance affecting both the value of the equity asset and the dividends (profit). And the reason is simpler than you might imagine. Consumers are fickle; they change their minds about what to buy on a whim. Businesses serving consumers can be affected very quickly by changes in the marketplace. Competition, trends, fashions, commodity prices, interest rates, elections, consumer sentiment, even the weather can have an immediate impact on a business's performance, and in doing so affect the profit of an equity investment.

While these things can and do affect property prices and rents, it takes much longer for such changes to take place. Also, there are generally fewer available substitutes for property. Moving house takes time, and we all have to live somewhere. Changing warehouses also takes a business time. Shutting a factory is no easy task, and even retail (probably the most volatile sector in property) isn't immune to forces that make it difficult to close a store. But with equity, many things people spend on are discretionary, meaning we can choose not to buy them or to buy fewer of them and generally tighten our belts. So equity usually commands a higher return on the money invested to take into account the heightened risk. Similarly, equity stakes in consumer staples (think food) are usually safer because people have little choice but to buy such goods. Very well established large businesses and brands tend to be less volatile because they reach wider and deeper into people's wallets.

Equity, in a business or a portion of a business we own, has two important sub-categories: *passive capital* and *active capital*. Passive capital is money we invest in a company or business that we don't control, that is not ours, or where we don't have any say in its decision making or operations. This includes investment funds and direct share investing. It's the act of entrusting our money to others (hopefully with a history of providing good returns to investors) so they can grow the money on our behalf.

Active capital is money we invest in our own ventures. We put money down hoping to make a profit from the activity. It could be as simple as opening a store on eBay to something as complex as starting a manufacturing company. It's the act of being an entrepreneur, regardless of the size of the venture, which defines active capital.

Anyone who wants to be successful at equity investing always has a better chance of success when they play in both the active and passive capital spaces. Knowledge in one informs the other. If you've run your own business, or faced the challenges of starting a venture, it's far easier to assess passive investment realistically.

All of these types of storage places can be called on, or converted back into money, and have the potential to generate more money while it is being stored. Even cash can generate small returns if held in bank deposits. But the key distinction we need to remember between the three places we can put our money is how differently they behave around *accessibility, return* and *risk*.

These, of course, relate to expectations over time (see table 7.1) and, as with any investment, unexpected results can and do occur.

Table 7.1: money storage — accessibility, return and risk

Money storage	Cash	Property	Equity
Accessibility	High	Low	Medium–high
Return	Low–negative	Medium–high	Medium–high
Risk	Low	Low–medium	Medium

This much can be said about property and equity: if, over the long term, you put your money into these things, instead of into stuff, you'll end up with lots of money. The money tends to go up in value. When it doesn't go up, and you lose it, it hurts a lot, but you tend to move up the learning curve really quickly, so it doesn't happen too often. It reminds me of the two investment rules of the world's greatest investor, Warren Buffett:

» Rule number one: Never lose capital invested.

» Rule number two: Refer to rule number one.

But my basic rule is this: if we want financial freedom, then we have to accumulate money, and the two best ways to do that are to accumulate property and equity.

Where to allocate our dollars

I hope we've all agreed that saving is key, and you've kept reading since I challenged you on discriminating between necessities and luxuries, so, bottom line, what do we do with our dollars? How should we allocate the money we earn in percentage terms?

The following basic formula, applied to every dollar earned, will create maximum opportunities for financial freedom. This is still the best economic model I know. It's *the 70/30 money rule*:

» 70 per cent to live on

» 30 per cent to save and invest.

We should never spend more than 70 per cent of the money we earn. We need to learn to live on 70 per cent of our income and to save 30 per cent. Sounds like a lot. But there's a very good chance you used to know how to do it but you've just forgotten. This is especially so if you've been working for a few years. When you used to earn less money than you do now, you somehow managed to get by, and to live a good life. You may even look back on those days fondly, even though you probably earned a lot less than you do now. A simple calculation shows that a pay rise of 3 per cent per year equates to a 31 per cent income hike over 10 years. We all managed to survive on what we earned in the past, so we know we can do it, but all too often we upgrade our living standards in direct alignment with our income increases. We're all guilty of it. When our income goes up, we get a nicer car, we go to nicer restaurants, we buy fancy takeaway coffee, nicer clothes, our holidays are a little bit more luxurious. And we deserve it, right? We worked hard to get it! So now it's a simple choice only we can make, but people who have more discipline now always end up with far more than they expect later.

If you're a little older, like me (I've been out of school for more than 20 years), the 30 per cent might seem like too much. If it is, and you are serious, then there are a couple of things you can do. The first port of call should be to think about what financial commitments you can cut loose. Do you really need that Netflix subscription? How much data does your phone need? Could you downgrade your car? Spend less on going out? I promise you there are more nice-to-haves on the expenses side of your ledger than you imagine. If you don't believe me, do this exercise to prove me wrong: For one month, write down every single dollar you spend and where it went. I promise you'll be surprised by how much of your spending is, well, let's say 'optional'.

If you're a little younger, not like me, start the habit now while the numbers are small. Don't get into the habit of living it up before you've earned the right financially. If you start young, the 70/30 rule will make you a laureate in the major of economics.

The easiest hack for saving 30 per cent is to put it where you can't touch it the moment you receive it. Some people call this 'paying yourself first', which is a great way to express it. In this sense, we define pay not as the lump sum we get at the end of the week or month, but as the amount we put aside. That's the bit for us, because quite literally the other money (the 70 per cent) is going to go all over the place to pay other people. It's going to pay the grocery store, the landlord or bank mortgage, the electricity company, the clothing store, the café. Everyone else will get their pay from what we earn, so we need to flip it in our favour by paying ourselves first, literally. It also makes it much harder to spend money that isn't easily accessible. This is why it's vital that it goes into a 'future fund'. I learned a long time ago a difference in attitude between people who become financially independent and people who don't. The key difference in behaviour is this:

Financially independent people pay themselves first and spend what's left.

People who struggle financially spend first and save what's left.

Those who spend first and save as an afterthought rarely have anything left to save. They struggle because they have the order back to front, not because of how much or little they earn.

If you've studied your expenses and it just isn't possible for you right now, hold onto the principle but modify the numbers. Maybe for you a 90/10 ratio is an achievable way to get the good habit started. Or if you've overcommitted yourself financially and are in debt and in really bad shape, maybe 99/1 is the best you can manage. But at least then you're in the game, and a better pattern becomes set. What really matters is the principle of setting savings aside. It's important here, though, that you don't cheat yourself by putting aside less than you can. Doing less than you can always messes with your ego.

Of course, this advice is for mature people, for people who want to be honest with themselves so as to set up their future. It takes a mature mindset to understand the truth about money. It might sound like cultural heresy to claim that everyone can do this. I'm aware of that, and I'm saying it anyway because I know it's true and it's still possible in these tough times to get ahead. Even people who have dug themselves into a deep hole can start small by setting themselves minimum viable savings (MVS).

The 30 per cent split

The 30 per cent is split equally among the three places money can be stored — cash, equity and property:

» 10 per cent cash

» 10 per cent property

» 10 per cent equity.

Cash will be allocated for emergency safety money, cash in the bank and easily accessible funds. This is for unexpected expenses or in case of emergency. The good thing, of course, is that if no unexpected expenditure is needed, then the savings can be redirected to the two other storage categories.

Property will go into a future fund. This should be put aside for future investments in property. It will take some time before you can buy or invest in a property, but that's what this fund is for.

Equity will go into an account earmarked for investment in shares (passive capital) or starting a business of your own (active capital). This category is a bit different from property in that it doesn't take much money to start investing. Anyone can buy a few hundred dollars' worth of shares or investment funds electronically through most banks. Your first entrepreneurial venture could be selling a few items online or offering your services on a digital platform. Ways to get started with active capital and inventing money are covered in Part III, 'Reinvention'.

You might be wondering why you don't just save 30 per cent and keep it in one account, so reducing the complexity a little. Here's why: the *habit* is what matters most. We want to get you thinking about your economic life as a portfolio of options. Options that make you future proof. Even if the amounts are small, this new approach, which creates a portfolio of investments, is the start of becoming bulletproof no matter what the economic conditions. It stimulates the mind to the possibilities. You can watch the amounts add up in each account and get excited about what you can do with these funds. It's an important part of the change in mindset from being a subservient wage earner to becoming self-reliant. It feels incredible and builds confidence. It's the start of taking control.

It's bigger than you

Saving habits matter because they have the added benefit of creating access to more money. It's not just important for you personally; it's how the people who control the money make decisions. Your banker never asks to see your school report! Neither does a venture capitalist or an investor in your business.

What they both want to see is your financial score card, and it's a pretty basic thing. They want to see how much money you generate and how much you set aside. They'll use different terms and forms, but that's what they're interested in. If you can show them your good habits, then they're more likely to decide you're a good risk for them to take with their money. People invest in your habits more than anything else. It's as true for money, for job interviews and for startup investors as it is for most things across the economic landscape.

CHAPTER 8
The future of money

Money tends to follow certain laws of attraction. It is especially attracted to things that are scarce but much in demand. So in order to attract more of it, we must understand how technology is changing the scarcity equation. The first part of this equation is how easy something is to do. The easier a skill is to learn, the less scarce it will be, because more people will come forward and offer to do it. To determine where more money will be earned, we need to look at what things technology is making scarce and what things technology is making abundant.

Our financial future depends on putting ourselves on the side of scarcity. While a lot of industries won't admit it, once technology makes some roles abundant, the business model of that industry (including employment, earning and investment prospects) is never the same again. Quite often the industry or company will refuse to admit the truth that their glory days are behind them. It doesn't mean you have to. If you see the ship is sinking for a certain industry, or a company you work for (and don't own), then you should jump ship as soon as possible. Companies deserve as much loyalty as they'll give you in tough times, and that's exactly none. Companies tell you that their most important asset is their people, and this is true. What they don't tell you is that their people are interchangeable, disposable and will come and go over time.

The company isn't real

Never forget that a company isn't real. It's a semi-fictional construct created by people with the goal of accumulating money while removing their personal and legal risk. It's not a person, a body, or anything real or human, as they often claim. In many ways companies are a bit like a virus. They establish themselves inside a host (the market). If they are successful, the number of the cells inside it (employees) grows. If the virus does well it spreads to other hosts (new markets). Cells within the virus might reproduce or die (employees come and go). The only thing that matters to the virus is self-perpetuation. It doesn't care about its host (companies will happily pollute the market) or the cells it's made of (so long as there are enough to get the job done). It only cares that it continues to exist. If that means that the host or the cells get 'damaged', it doesn't care, so long as it continues to thrive and reproduce.

I'm not anti-corporate, I'm just a truth merchant. Many of the people I've met in these corporations remain my best friends. But I want you to be able to see the reality of the system we all operate in, to help you navigate it from a human perspective and achieve a good return on humanity (ROH). I've spent a large part of my career working for big corporations (think Fortune 500) in the fast-moving consumer goods world. When I finally arrived at the level of managing people directly, one of the first things I would tell them is this:

'The company we work for does not care about us. They don't care about me, and they don't care about you. I'll try to help you, as a person, in your career. If that means you need to work elsewhere, I'll help you get to that better place. If it means

I need to be more loyal to you than to the company we work for, I'll do that too. If your goal is to exit the corporate world and finally get moving on that business you want to start, tell me how I can help. I'm here for you. In the end, companies come and go; we'll be inside one for a period, and then we're gone. And the company won't care; it'll carry on as if we'd never existed. The thing that really matters, while we are here working for this company, is each other. Our relationships will outlast the companies we work for, so let's look after each other first. And if we do this, the companies we work for will be beneficiaries anyway.'

This may sound counterintuitive, or even disloyal, but in my experience it's the starting point of true loyalty and better outcomes in a business or project of any size. I cared about the people who worked for me, and did whatever I could for them, as people — and for the company second. In the end the company always benefited more than you might expect from this anti-corporate approach. Sometimes it's worth remembering what really matters as we play this 'unreal' game of corporate oligopoly, and that is that we look after each other first.

SO WHEN IT COMES TO LOYALTY, BE LOYAL TO YOURSELF AND TO YOUR FRIENDS IN THE COMPANY. THE COMPANY ITSELF IS EPHEMERAL AND EXISTS ONLY AS A FINANCIAL CONSTRUCT.

The 'turnaround' hoax

There's one more thing that's important to mention in these times of rapid change. Don't try to be a hero — avoid the turnaround job. I'm talking about work, employment and sometimes even entrepreneurial opportunities to fix broken companies and industry business models. Yes, occasionally a hero arrives who saves the company and the day, but this is so rare that we know the names of the handful of people who have pulled it off. Unless this is a passion project, and it matters to you deeply on a visceral level, I'd avoid it at all costs. Our economic life is tough enough without trying to solve the problems of a company in deep trouble. And given the fact that they'll be highly unlikely to help you when *you're* in deep trouble, it's not worth trying to do a corporate rescue job.

A much smarter life strategy is to work in an industry whose tide is rising, because a rising tide floats all boats. Again, this might sound mercenary, but if you're in an industry that's starting to struggle, get out and go where the business model is working better. It's far more profitable to be an average performer on board a winning ship than a star on a sinking ship. Companies doing well pay more, they invest in and educate their staff more, and they get into a positive spiral of profit, which they invest in tomorrow. If the industry you work in is touted to be disrupted, it probably will be. If you can see that it faces potential decline, cross over to the industry that is eating it up. Learn the new skills they want and add them to the valuable skills you already have. It's not worth trying to work out a survival plan, especially for a corporation. A far better option is to go somewhere else where growth is strong and the future is bright.

If you're still not convinced, just remember this about any large corporation you might work for. If something terrible happens and a staff member dies, of course everyone who works there will be devastated by the news. The company will support the staff, and in some ways the unfortunate person's family too. After all, chances are they have paid their insurance. Flowers and condolences will be sent. But the same day the news comes through, as ugly as this sounds, the company will start planning their replacement. They may even advertise for the position that has opened up. It's not evil, it's just what companies are and do. Put yourself first. You owe it to yourself and your family.

The future value equation

The value equation in the future will pretty much be where it was in the past, and that is around things that are both valued and scarce. The change is only in the context — in what has become scarce. In the past it used to be difficult to make things and easy to sell them. In a world of abundance, this model has been turned upside down. It's now much easier to make things, and much more difficult to find a market for them. Just look at the availability of the tools of production. Anyone can get cheap manufacturing done for them in China through Alibaba.com. Anyone can get software built on their behalf by finding people with the skills needed using one of the myriad outsourcing websites. Anyone can get products shipped overseas in 24 hours or transfer funds globally in an instant with a few clicks.

In the industrial era, making things efficiently was a winning business strategy and people who attached themselves to these value providers got a good share of the pie. Now the game is about connection. Indeed, this revolution is about connection more than it is about technology. It's a connection revolution underpinned by new technological capabilities. The scarcest thing in today's society is attention. Where people's attention is divided, who gets it, and what products and services command it, can be instructive as to where the scarcity equation is moving to. People who want to attract money and future-proof their personal revenue streams would do well to pay attention to the shifts in abundance and scarcity:

» *Becoming abundant and cheap:* All information, entertainment, news, transport, clothing through fast fashion, mapping, intelligence (through AI), computer screens, consumer goods, shipping and logistics, manufacturing (labour, 3D printing etc.), electronic data.

» *Becoming scarce and valuable:* People's attention, our privacy, physical space, access to nature, face-to-face contact, personal service, curation of valuable content, interface design, service design, craftwork, filtering of data, making sense of data points, human performance, art, creativity.

Unions—the false friend

Here's what unions do in a sentence. They slowly and painfully put their members out of work. Unions are status quo machines in a world where the natural trajectory and evolution of technology cares nothing for the status quo. Unions are a very interesting case as we exit the industrial economy. Their value was historically created through the scarcity of skilled labour and the corporations' need for labour to function. When labour organised itself through unions, it created a heightened level of quasi 'invented scarcity'. Tight unions could form an all-or-nothing barrier that organisations just had to negotiate with. This was especially so before the era of hyper-globalisation. If the company didn't negotiate and come to terms with a union the corporation reliant on union members could come to a complete halt.

Unions have historically had their place. They made workplaces safer, more human, they stopped child labour, regulated working hours and made their industries more civilised. In addition, the union would negotiate wages for its members, often in line with profit improvements or efficiency gains. The problem is the unions always priced themselves out of the market. If labour was the only option, this made sense; it was, and it did. But as the price of labour goes up, the company will look to alternatives. In globalised markets with low trade barriers, the manufacturing goes offshore to lower-cost labour markets; in an age of robotics and AI, the work goes to automation. The union may get more money for its members in the short term, but they ensure their members end up being replaced sooner than they otherwise would be. It never works out in the long run.

Unions would do better to help members upskill and reskill over long periods of inevitable transition. They'd do better to create more value for members than to act adversarially towards the corporations they negotiate with. When the corporation had no option but to hire 'people', the union strategy worked; now, as if by stealth, 'expensive labour' is simply replaced by machines, and the unions have no recourse. When people put their faith in a union, they are outsourcing responsibility to a quickly evaporating business model.

It's not a good financial or life strategy to use tactical games to get more than the market wants to give; it just never works out. A better strategy is to try to become more valuable than you are, rather than to extract more value for what you already do. If unions had been smart, they would have expanded their market more broadly into the white-collar world. When I worked in the corporate world my dad used to laugh at me being a white-collar worker, spending long hours of the day and night in the office trying to get work done and get ahead. He reckoned highly educated office workers have become a 'white-collar underclass', citing the days when office workers never did overtime, because that was for poor blue-collar workers and tradesmen like him. He said that back then the office workers zipped home at 4.30 every day while lower-paid workers stayed back to earn a bit more. He had a point. Now the corporate hierarchy climber has a fixed salary yet is expected to put in a few extra hours of unpaid work. It says so in every employment contract. It goes something like this:

'Occasionally, you'll be required to work beyond the formal eight hours a day as part of your existing salary package ...'

Too bad they don't tell you it's every other day, and sometimes until midnight to finish that report or business plan that no one really cares about and won't win one more customer. (Sorry, couldn't help myself. I did so many of these back in the day and I wanted to share the pain!) Anyway, we can't leave the office before the boss, right? It looks bad. Even if you've got nothing to do, better to surf the net, call some friends and fit into the office culture. Looks like my dad was right.

And this one is my favourite of all time — the sushi stooge! Work at Google or technology startup XYZ and get free food, free dry cleaning, a gym in the office, massages on Friday and airline-style, first-class sleeping pods. It's the greatest corporate trick of all time. Take engineers worth $100/hour, give them $12 worth of sushi and get them working all night. Sometimes the most important thing we can do in our financial lives is to honestly view the world as it is. Yes, it's great to get benefits, but sometimes the price is too high.

CHAPTER 9
The best way to invest money

There's an infinite number of ways we can invest. I'm not going to set out a detailed plan here, but instead I'll offer something more valuable, based on fundamental investing principles that are unchanged by time or technological shifts. Understand these principles and you'll be able to determine the merits of any investment proposition you may consider in future. I've read all the investment classics and the modern discourses on the subject. What follows is a distillation of the best information I have gleaned from these sources. It will include a few clear, unambiguous recommendations on strategies I've used to create financial independence, where to get more information on them and how to get started.

I read and studied share and property investing for many years after I left school. I was completely obsessed with this incredible, life-changing knowledge. Such valuable information had never made it into the classroom, of course. I probably would have got quicker results if we'd been taught about this stuff at school. 'Get Rich 101' — now that's a class even the rebellious kids would have signed up for! It has been some of the most valuable information I've ever absorbed. In fact, understanding about investing doesn't just help you grow your money; it helps you understand the world and business generally. Knowing this stuff made me a far better entrepreneur and corporate executive. It has even helped me understand the nuances of political decision making.

This chapter offers a brief survey of the simplest investment methods used to provide solid investment returns that will enrich anyone who has the discipline to follow them. The advice is not based on my own inventiveness; rather, it represents the accumulated wisdom of some of the world's greatest investors. I'm simply passing their ideas on.

Time and money—the two investments we make

Investing isn't just for the rich. People on modest incomes can invest too. I'd even argue that the lucky trust fund babies aren't really investors so much as recipients of large donations. I learned early not to envy people born with financial wealth, because they miss out on the adventure of learning and following the path to building their own financial independence, a wonderful journey to take.

Anyone can choose to be an investor, because we can only ever invest two things, time and money. If we don't have money, then we must invest time — time in the form of labour and time in planning how to keep some of that money we've 'earned'. Then, as we start to accumulate more money, we need to invest more time in educating ourselves. This can be to acquire larger amounts of earned money but also to learn more about investing.

Time and money are interesting assets. Unlike money, time can't be divided or traded to other people and it doesn't compound; it remains static, and what isn't used is wasted. So we need to give it the respect it deserves.

Most of us start out investing time. We do this through part-time or full-time jobs, schooling and self-education. We invest our time making and building things for a small business or startup we are bootstrapping. Using our time to make something — a product or a service — that we can sell at a profit is one of the greatest ways to generate money. It's what most real entrepreneurs who aren't living in the Silicon Valley non-reality bubble actually do. They use what skills and resources they have at their disposal today to create something, to make something happen, and to sell it. They do it one customer at a time, and they build on that to make money. They aren't out there trying to generate vanity metrics.[13]

Before we have excess *money* to invest we must first invest in ourselves. Thereafter the principle is simple: When we don't have enough money, we invest more time. When we don't have enough time, we invest more money. Eventually we want to use money to invent time for doing whatever it is that creates value in our lives and in the lives of those around us.

We assess what we have of each asset to generate more of the other. In some ways, time is of greater value and wealth should be measured in time rather than money. This is because time is a type of freedom. It is the only asset we can't accumulate more of, so we should do what we can to preserve it.

MONEY IS VALUABLE NOT JUST BECAUSE IT CAN BUY STUFF, BUT BECAUSE IT CAN INVENT TIME, GIVING US MORE OF THE MOST VALUABLE THING ON EARTH.

The basics are beautiful

The less you know about investing, the better you'll be at it, or, more precisely, the simpler the investment choices you will make. And the less complex your investing methods, the more

129

money you'll make. Anyone who truly understands passive capital knows this, including the greatest investor of all time, Warren Buffett.

Complex investment tools rarely generate the returns they promise, and their very complexity often turns them into devices for transferring money from the buyer of said investment vehicles to the seller. The dumber the money, the smarter it becomes. The maintenance of simplicity in an investment strategy tends to make the investment easier to understand; it most often reduces the cost of making the investment, and it ensures that we are rational investors and not gamblers trying to beat the system. As you've read so far, the system is hard — sometimes impossible — to beat. The best strategy is to use the system to your own advantage by knowing its flaws.

The best way to get an above-average return is really very simple. By being an investor you put yourself in the top 10 per cent of people in the first place, because most people just never get around to it. This is confirmed by the fact that 66 per cent of retirees in Australia live on government subsidies and pensions. Then, by knowing how to do it well, effectively and simply, you elevate yourself further into the top 10 per cent of investors. And just like that, with enough time, you'll become a one percenter (in my world, this is someone who knows more than 99 per cent of people in their subject area. More on that on p171).

The main challenges to investing

The main challenges to investing money successfully come down to what I call the three P's:

» probability

» price

» patience.

1. PROBABILITY

This is the likelihood that the revenue that underpins the investment will remain stable for a long enough period of time. Even in times of great technological disruption there are certain ways to invest that just don't change. When Amazon founder Jeff Bezos looks for ways to grow his business, he doesn't try to guess the future; instead, he asks himself: 'What's not going to change in the next 10 years? You can build a business strategy around the things that are stable in time ... In our retail business, we know that our customers want low prices, and I know that's going to be true 10 years from now. They want fast delivery; they want a vast selection. It's impossible to imagine a future 10 years from now where a customer comes up and says; "Jeff, I love Amazon; I just wish the prices were a little higher" [or] "I love Amazon; I just wish you'd deliver a little more slowly." Impossible.'[14]

So too for investing. It's a game of going for high probability, not high returns. The compounding effect of high-probability events is the factor that creates high returns for investors. Think about it like this: if you make one bad investment in which you lose your money, it will take 10 further investments at a solid return of 10 per cent just to get back to where you started.

2. PRICE

This is the cost of acquiring and maintaining the investment. Investment tools with high fees absolutely decimate most investments people make. When the costs of making an investment are high, you start by making a loss, which sounds as ridiculous as it is. The best investments are made using simple, low-cost vehicles. Most solid, long-term investments generally will return 10 per cent per annum. The S&P 500, which represents the top 500 public companies in the world, has averaged a return of 9 per cent over the past 144 years, 10.2 per cent over the past 100 years, 9.7 per cent over the past 50 years,

9.3 per cent over the past 25 years, 7.6 per cent over the past 10 years and 12.9 per cent over the past five years.[15] The return for a *patient and diversified* investment is not about to change from around 10 per cent anytime soon. Consider, of course, that these periods have covered every kind of economic, social and political upheaval imaginable, including wars, depressions, famines and the recent GFC.

Residential property has had similar investment returns of about 10 per cent per annum over the long run. Australian property prices have grown at 10.4 per cent over the past 120 years, while in the UK, where records go back almost 1000 years, property has risen at a compound rate of 10.2 per cent over nearly a millennium.[16] It's almost as if this 10 per cent number is some kind of force of nature. And 10 per cent is a wonderful number; when we take into account the compounding returns, it really adds up.

The 'Rule of 72' states that if you divide the number 72 by the annual growth rate you are expecting, you can see how long it will take to double your money. Give it a try. With a return of 10 per cent, the investment will double in 7.2 years, and double again in another 7.2 years. In under 15 years, with what the market regards as an 'average' return, $100 000 would become $400 000. I'd say, when applied rationally, the 'average' could be your best friend and make your financial position anything but average. And the reason is simple: most people don't have the discipline to achieve those average results.

As noted, the costs associated with your investment can have a dramatic impact. Having an investment vehicle eat up 2, 3 or 5 per cent, which is not uncommon, reduces the average return by 50 per cent. Imagine if you had to give away half your net wage! Half of the investing money game is keeping costs low. The other half is having the patience to let the returns compound. This is something only those with excess savings can ever do; everyone else is too financially constrained to be patient, and all too often they take unnecessary risks trying to make up lost ground.

3. PATIENCE

It is smart to be impatient with certain things in life, but investing is not one of them. The compound effect that annual returns can have on investments is what makes people rich. The only way to get compound returns is by holding an investment for a prolonged time. Even if we trade (buy and sell) investments, our returns are eaten into by taxation. In Australia only investments held for more than 12 months receive the 50 per cent taxation rate discount. Mathematical concepts are sometimes difficult to get our head around; compounding is a bit like that. One way to think of it is that the return on investment gets bigger the longer we hold it, because we always pay *yesterday's* price. In each new year, the return a company makes usually gets added to its value, so the people who bought it earlier get more money back over time. Table 9.1 (overleaf) illustrates the effects of interest that compounds at 10 per cent per annum on an initial investment of $1000.

Merely by holding onto the investment, the ROI goes up every year — look at column 5. By year 7 you are generating a 17.7 per cent ROI, the sort of return usually reserved for the world's greatest investors, just by being patient. You've doubled your original investment after 7.2 years.

The second reason patience is vital is that very few things in life move in a straight line. Most investment returns don't follow a straight line either; they bounce around a trajectory or general direction. Look at the chart in figure 9.1 (on page 135) roughly showing the US sharemarket over the past five years. While the return has been steady, it has been a bumpy ride.

It's easy to see it's heading up over time, but there are negative days, weeks, months and even years. This is why patience is

Table 9.1: the effects of compounding interest

Year	Amount invested	Return on investment	Gain for the year	Return on original investment	New value of investment
Year 1	$1000	10%	$100	10%	$1100
Year 2	$1100	10%	$110	11%	$1210
Year 3	$1210	10%	$121	12.1%	$1331
Year 4	$1331	10%	$133	13.3%	$1464
Year 5	$1464	10%	$146	14.6%	$1611
Year 6	$1611	10%	$161	16.1%	$1772
Year 7	$1772	10%	$177	17.7%	$1949
Year 8	$1949	10%	$195	19.5%	$2144
Year 9	$2144	10%	$214	21.4%	$2358
Year 10	$2358	10%	$236	23.6%	$2594

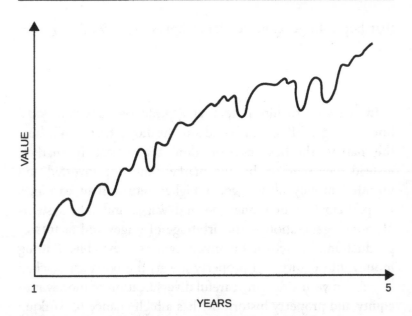

Figure 9.1: the US sharemarket over the past 5 years

key. You need to ride the bumps. The annual returns on the S&P 500, an index that tracks the top 500 stocks and is a good representation of the overall sharemarket, show that the past five years have produced returns of 2 per cent, 16 per cent, 32 per cent, 14 per cent and 1 per cent.[17] In some periods the index will fall dramatically in certain years, so we need to invest for solid periods of time — five years minimum, but the longer the better. It's time in the market that counts. Trying to time the good years is not worth the risk.

Mistaking gambling for investing

Often people mistake gambling for investing, even in traditional investing realms such as shares and property.

The shorter the period of time you are prepared to wait for your return, the more likely it is that you are gambling. A lotto ticket, a horse race, an evening at the casino — any investment that hopes to generate results in hours, days, weeks or even months is most likely speculation at best, gambling at worst. Investing is a game of years, when the law of averages works for you and compounding returns can make miracles.

Even trying to flip a stock at a profit because you got a hot tip is gambling. It's based on the hope that you'll beat the market. The best investors don't try to beat the market; instead they seek to 'be' the market, knowing invested and invented money always get a higher return than earnings. By participating in money beyond wages and into systems of money generation — the arbitrage of wages and factors of production — a return on investment is inevitable. Putting money into equity and property means the odds are stacked heavily on your side. Any careful diversification of money into equity and property historically has a high chance of working out. Intuitively we know when we are gambling. We know when we are taking a risk to get a quick and bigger than usual return. Often it is just about being honest with ourselves. Knowing the house always wins in any form of gambling should be enough to discourage recklessness. We all work way too hard to take foolish risks trying to get higher than usual returns. I can't stress highly enough that this applies to buying shares too.

The success bias

When it comes to investing, the media can distort reality. We need to remember that it's in the nature of the media to report anomalies, not just in the negative stories they specialise in but in the good news story too. They tend to report stories of unusual, against-the-odds success, which makes us believe in fantasy. Inordinate returns on an investment will be reported, because it's a more interesting story than one headed, 'Hear the boring story of how one investor got rich slowly following predictable returns on basic shares and residential property'. There's very little clickbait value in that story, but it's the one that will make you rich. The same can be said for the story of any startup founder who ended up building a billion-dollar business.

It's a poor plan to bank on the improbable when it comes to investing and inventing money through entrepreneurship. The reason we know these stories is because of the success bias. The one-in-a-1000 success is reported; the 999 people who employed the same flawed strategy and lost it all are never written about — because their story doesn't sell. And remember, these stories are in the business of selling hope, and laziness, not truth. Attention goes to the winner, even if winning in that way is unlikely. Outsized returns can happen, but they need to be part of a smaller portion of a portfolio approach.

What makes investments go up in value

The most important lesson in economics is the first one we learn: demand and supply.

Increasing demand for the thing you invest in indicates the price will go up over time. If more people want the thing you hold — say, a property or the use of that property — or a company is selling more of its product than it sold last year, this will drive up demand. The reverse, of course, is that when supply of something increases, people have more options on where to get a substitute, and this creates downward pressure. Here are the most basic questions we can ask ourselves before we invest in anything: Is the demand for this product, service or property likely to continue? What is the probability of substitutes arriving? Are the barriers to others seeing the profit and entering the game high or low? How unique is it? One reason residential property can be such a great investment is that it is easy for the layperson to understand the investment and see its value through their own eyes.

Another great way to assess the value of an investment is the yield. The yield is the percentage return you receive in terms of rent or dividends/profit share:

» *Rent:* The higher the percentage this is of the purchase price, the 'cheaper' the asset has been to buy. But it is more important to know if this yield is likely to be maintained, or even increased, over time. If the renter leaves, would it be easy to rent out again? This is the all-important question. The same for selling: would it be easy to sell? Before you invest, regardless of how cheap it would be to buy based on the yield, the answer to this question ought always to be *yes*.

» *Profit/dividends:* The same question applies here, but on aggregate. Is the company likely to find as many customers next year as this year? Will they be able to maintain their prices and/or reduce costs? Do they have new services/products in the pipeline? Is it easy to sell the investment to another buyer quickly? Most blue-chip companies pass this test.

We should be happy with the returns we get from any investment from day one, so we profit at purchase. We should be confident the return will continue and grow and that there is a high probability the asset will be in demand for years to come.

The two best passive investments you can make are index investing and residential property investing.

INTRODUCTION TO INDEX INVESTING

Remember how we defined gambling: as trying to beat the averages by guessing and taking a high risk? Well, index investing is about *being* the average.

Index investing is the idea that we buy 'the entire share market'. Now before you dismiss this as crazy, you need to remember a couple of things: most people never invest, other than through their superannuation or 401k; and money is a game of relativity — it's about having more than the average, not the most. So an average return over a long time will make you richer than most people. It's also about probability and patience. With index investing, we get all the winners and ditch all the losers. By doing so, our returns are rounded off, we won't get the highs that come with picking a winning stock, like Google or Tesla when they floated, but it also means we don't get burned by a Kodak going down in flames. When we invest in an index, an investment firm buys *all* the stocks in an index such as the S&P 500 in the proportion of the market they represent. So if Apple is 3 per cent of the index, then 3 per cent of your holdings will be in Apple shares, and so on. They do this for the top 500 stocks. When a stock drops to number 501, the index will sell it; likewise, when a stock rises to 500, the index will invest in it. By doing this, an index can replicate the average return of the market based on that index for you. You do as well as the market, and we've already seen that over time it does well.

Because it's a system that doesn't require frequent trading or paying some high-flyer on Wall Street to pick stocks, the fees and taxes are much lower on this type of investment, further boosting its returns. The crazy thing is that over the long term there isn't one investment fund that has beaten the index. I know, crazy! Yes, every year there are funds, and individual investors too, that beat the index, but very few manage to repeat the feat. Investing is for long-game players, and this is the best long game in town. Warren Buffett himself, the second richest person in the world and, as we've noted, the greatest investor of all time, recommends index investing, and has decided to allocate 90 per cent of his wealth to this investment methodology[18] after his death.

The best place to make such an investment is with Vanguard Investments. I'd recommend buying into the S&P 500 because it gives global exposure through the largest and most successful companies operating around the world. It also has the breadth to cover the disruption that is happening in many industries. As companies fall out, new heroes will come in, and you'll own them by default. By investing in an index like this, you can expect to get returns of around 10 per cent per annum, as we saw earlier, so long as you stay in the market for at least five years, although the longer you stay in the better. The minimum investment amount to buy into an index is $5000, after which additions of as little as $100 can be made.

I've long been a fan of indexing. I did a detailed podcast on it almost 10 years ago, and all the principles remain true to this day. You can listen to it at: stevesammartino.com/indexinvesting.

Going deeper

If you want to go deep on the subject of index investing and why it is the best method of share investing, then I'd recommend one book (and I've read them all): *A Random Walk Down Wall Street* by Burton G. Malkiel.

If you're looking for a general share investing book, then *The Intelligent Investor* by Benjamin Graham should be on your list.

INTRODUCTION TO RESIDENTIAL PROPERTY INVESTING

Residential property is a bit like index investing in property markets. It depends on the wider economic performance. In most developed markets the return on investment has been around 10 per cent, but it's been much higher in Australia recently. Most of us understand how residential property investment works. We buy a property and collect rent on it to help pay off the capital. In Australia you can expect to get a rental return of around 2 per cent comfortably. There are significant tax benefits and you only need to make up the gap between the rent and the interest cost to hold onto an investment that has historically grown at 10 per cent. The kicker with residential property investing is that banks will often lend large sums of money on property — as high as 90 per cent of the property's value. Which means you get leverage. If you bought a property with a 10 per cent deposit and it went up in value by 10 per cent, then in valuation terms you've doubled your money in a year. This is one of the reasons it's such a popular investment tool.

There's a lot to residential property investing, and some of the paths can be risky, especially in Australia where we've had unprecedented value growth without a hitch for many years. The barriers to entry are also a bit higher than with shares. So if you're keen, I recommend just one book: *The Millionaire Real Estate Investor* by Gary Kelly. This book is now more than 10 years old, so some of the numbers will be dated, but the principles don't change. It's the best how-to guide for a novice I've read, and again, I've read them all.

Financial independence

Definitions matter so much in life. They can be an important reminder of the *what* and *why*, especially why we are really doing something. They're also something we need to reassess over time, because language is living and organic, and definitions change quickly and without notice. This means a definition we have long held close to our hearts may no longer be true. By not assessing what something really means today, we might end up following a path that makes no sense for us. *Financial independence* is a term we hear a lot but rarely challenge ourselves to define. Here's a definition worth remembering:

FINANCIAL INDEPENDENCE IS THE ABILITY TO LIVE FROM ONE'S OWN RESOURCES, WITHOUT THE UNDUE INFLUENCE OR INTERFERENCE OF OTHERS.

I believe this is a fundamental right we all should aim for, and we should help to empower others to achieve the same goal. I also believe that in our omni-connected society, people who make this possible for others in a collaborative sense using technology are far more likely to create it for themselves.

This definition allows us the flexibility to determine how we choose to live and what we regard as our own resources. So how do you know when you've got it? Well, there is a really good way to measure your progress towards financial independence. It's quite simple and a great way to assess how free you are from being 'told what to do' in life.

The financial wealth success ratio

We need to look at the ratio of *active* vs *passive money* we generate. This ratio tells the story of how much risk we have in earned money and wages and, in some ways, our dependence on systems we don't control. The equation looks like this:

Financial Wealth Ratio = Passive Income / Earned Income.

We should be aiming for a number that is greater than 1. The reason this is such an important formula is that it takes into account the most important and scarce resource — time. While it includes money, it goes beyond it. It indicates that earning money from control and ownership of assets is far superior to earning money through labour, regardless of how big the earned portion of our income may be. Earning passive income does not require our time.

So what is understood as passive income? It includes, but is not limited to, shares (dividends), business income (profits), property (rents), licensing rights (royalties) and any other assets we've acquired or built that put money in our pockets. It is *not* the net value of those assets, but what they generate in real returns — actual cash flow — just as a salary is a real return on our labour. And while trading large capital assets may generate actual cash returns, that return is singular and available only at the point of transaction. Unless we happen to be in the business of trading assets, it doesn't provide a true month-to-month reflection of our cash position. Passive income is about earnings and the probability of those earnings being maintained over time.

Why is passive income more important than earned income? Speaking of probability, another reason passive income is so vital is that it has a high probability of increasing. Rents and corporate earnings in most developed economies increase at around 10 per cent per annum. Wages, on the other hand, increase annually at less than 3 per cent per annum. Passive income also removes the power of others over us. When we earn wages, we are at the whim of the work environment, the company, our boss, the economy, technological upheaval and all manner of other factors that make having a job inferior.

EARNED INCOME IS RISKIER THAN PASSIVE INCOME BECAUSE IT GENERALLY IS NOT SOMETHING WE CONTROL.

Sure, we can influence it by becoming more skilled and valuable to the marketplace, but we can never have total decision-making authority, as we can when allocating our money to a portfolio.

A word of warning, though: 'Passive' income doesn't mean it shouldn't be actively managed, or that we don't need to earn money to acquire it. It takes effort, but it builds independence. In other words, a passive attitude doesn't build passive income; quite the opposite.

Passive income is the money we earn when we are not in the room. This is actually more important than total income. First, passive income usually grows over time. Rents go up — anyone who has rented a house knows this pattern. In good companies earnings increase over time. Second, passive income is important because it should be regarded as bonus money. We can manage to live on the earned portion of our income. We know this is true because most people start with zero passive income, unless they're a trust fund baby. The passive portion creates its own ecosystem in which it builds more of itself — think compound interest.

A STORY ABOUT THE STARS

Not those in the sky, but rock stars, sport stars and movie stars. There is no shortage of stories about such people going broke, bankrupt, after earning zillions of dollars. In fact, the statistics here are very telling. After two years' retirement, 78 per cent of NFL players are bankrupt or under severe financial stress. ESPN's '30 for 30' documentary *Broke* is worth watching on the topic. How is this even possible? The reason rock stars and sports stars go broke is that they have a poor financial ratio, pure and simple. They earn big, have bad spending habits and don't create a good financial wealth ratio while they have the chance. It should be easier for them than for anyone, but most don't take their opportunity. They don't de-risk their future.

A STORY ABOUT THE RICH

Look at any financially rich people you know, whether someone famous or a local businessperson you admire, and you'll see a good ratio. They own properties, have equity stakes in successful businesses and make most of their money from the passive side, rather than the earned. Even most employees who get rich — think CEOs — become so more from share options than from pure wages. The pattern is clear.

HOW TO HACK YOUR RATIO

The trick is to move money from the earned income denominator to the passive income nominator until at some point there is more passive than earned income, resulting in a ratio of 1 or higher. So long as we keep our spending in check, once we earn more money passively than actively, work (both type and frequency) becomes a choice. Another hack for building this equation in your favour is ensuring your earned income and passive income are in the same realm or industry. This usually gives you an advantage in your passive income building, as your skill base moves you up the learning curve of both sides of the wealth equation. This strategy often results in bigger earned and passive returns as they interact interdependently. Stick to what you know, and leverage that knowledge advantage to beat the averages.

KNOW YOUR RATIO

You need to know your position, your ratio, and to have a plan to increase the passive portion. The problem is that most people go through life aiming to increase the earned portion more than they do the passive portion. Lifestyle spending increases with income, so they end up with a micro version of the rock star problem. Knowing your ratio allows you to aim and game the system, and to set targets for increasing the passive side.

OTHER ADVANTAGES OF THE WEALTH EQUATION

In most economies the taxation system delivers large advantages to passive income. Often dividends are fully franked (the tax is already paid for you). You can offset your earned income with the expenses associated with generating your passive income. You don't have to pay tax as you earn this money (PAYE) and can earn interest on the returns before they are taxed. There are other structural benefits too, such as paying lower corporate tax rates through holding the passive income assets in a private company.

How to build passive income

Save at least 20 per cent of what you earn and invest it. As I've outlined in this chapter, the two simplest places to invest are residential property and index shares. Invest the ROI from the passive income in more passive income–generating assets — never spend any of it. If you can manage to do this, then as soon as your ratio is 1 or better, work becomes a choice rather than a necessity.

Add 'improve my wealth ratio' to your list of goals every year.

Capital always wins

Capital wins in a capitalist society. It just does. We've been dealt a hand that requires us to play by these rules if we want to create personal security, time with our families and the freedom to explore all that life offers. It doesn't mean that money is all that matters, just that it gives us options on how we spend our days and how much we have to rely on the whims of others. We can still choose to invest in what we see as ethical and provide value products and services to people at a fair price, like renting out a house that is well looked after to someone who needs it. In a world of choice, it's important we choose what is right for ourselves and those closest to us.

There's an entrepreneur buried deep down inside all of us. Maybe you're trying to find it, maybe you never lost it. There's never been a better time to change yourself and take control of your destiny, not just financially but in how you spend your days. Part III, 'Reinvention', will help you rekindle the flame that burned when you were a child. Boom.

Life-changing revenue hacks!

1. **There are three types of money — Earned, Invested and Invented.** They are not created equal. It is better to own and organise the factors of production than to be them.

2. **Earning money, or wages, is like carrying buckets of water.** The fuller your bucket, the more back-breaking the work. No matter how full the bucket, you only earn money when you are present. It's better to build a pipeline where the money flows through a system!

3. **People have careers, companies have jobs.** Be loyal to yourself first and honestly assess what is in your interest and what is in the company's interest.

4. **Profits are better than wages.** Never forget that every dollar you earn in profits becomes $2, $3, $10 or more in the asset you can sell. You can't sell your job.

5. **Everything starts with saving.** Financial greatness starts with the ability to save. If you cannot save, the seeds of greatness are not within you.

(Continued)

Life-changing revenue hacks! (Cont'd)

6. **There's no rule that says you can't work on your living and your financial independence at the same time.** You must pay yourself first to make this happen.

7. **Never think of money in hours of time; think of it rather as value created.** Hours and units are factory thinking; thinking in terms of value helps you maximise your true potential.

8. **Cash, property and equity all store money.** Putting money in the last two is the key to financial independence.

9. **Remember the 70/30 rule.** Never spend more than 70 per cent of what you earn and you'll be on the path to freedom.

10. **Average investment returns deliver wealth that is never average and often incredible.** The average person just doesn't invest. Ten per cent is a wonderful return on investment.

11. **Know your passive/earned income ratio.** Work on improving it every year. When it reaches 1, work becomes a choice rather than an obligation.

Part III
Reinvention

Both entrepreneurship and technology were once fringe activities. Saying you worked for yourself or you were an entrepreneur was often interpreted by the other party as admitting you were unemployed, or even unemployable, the last refuge of the unskilled and unwanted. So too with technology, that weird stuff nerds did late at night in garages with chemistry sets and soldering irons. Now these two activities are reshaping our economy and our futures, whether we pay attention to them or not. We must all upgrade our skills in these areas if we want to remain relevant and independent in the modern economy. No doubt you've got used to having to upgrade your technology devices and software. Every time that message pops up on our screen, we should ask ourselves, 'When was the last time I upgraded my own software? When did I last download a new module to make myself more useful and more in demand in the marketplace?'

Upgrading our grey matter is no longer a choice. It's a kind of ongoing economic hygiene check, in which small regular interventions ensure our long-term economic health. And it's easy to do if we do it regularly. It's a game of frequency, not depth. This last section of the book, 'Reinvention', is designed to show you the hacks you can use to make you as a person future proof, more so than any company you work for. You'll then have the choice of working for them or for yourself. These chapters will help you unlock the natural talents buried deep in your own humanity — the talent to explore, to try new things, to learn from your mistakes, to serve others, to use your imagination and to become a lot more entrepreneurial in your approach to life. You'll see how safe and low risk economic exploration can be, and how easy it is to leverage emerging technology using the skills you already have, because quite frankly, if you can read you can do it. The most difficult thing a human being can learn is language; when it comes to computational complexity, natural language processing is still up there at the top, so I know you can do it. You'll see how a little bit often can have a huge impact later. Here we need to remember the law of relatively: everyone can, but most people won't. Your success will depend on the effort you put in compared with others.

CHAPTER 10
Portfolio living

If you've ever tried to change industries or careers, you'll know how difficult the process can be. This is true even for roles that require no formal qualifications. The old 'experience' demon raises its head. They want someone with X years' industry experience, a person who has worked in clone conglomerate XYZ (probably their competitor), to fill the role that has just opened up. The recruiter — or increasingly these days the CV algorithmic short list generator — just wants to keep their customer happy, so they give them what they ask for. The hiring manager, well, they just want someone who can hit the ground running. Someone who knows the system, the rules, the game, the industry dynamics and business model. So they fill the office with clones and wonder why their industry and company is being disrupted!

It's not their fault, it's no one's fault, it's just the way companies and systems tend to evolve. What we need to do is be aware of it. It's why it's so hard to break into a new field. Everyone has been taught for so long that risk is bad and failure is bad that they don't want to bring in anyone who hasn't been vetted by the system. Sure, there are ways to hack your way into a new field, but the traditional method of doing it is ridiculously difficult. They say they want entrepreneurs and to act like startups, yet most won't even take the micro risk of employing someone who hasn't worked in that realm before.

Even companies that send you on training programs aren't doing it for you, they are doing it for them. It's a kind of software upgrade for their employees — a software patch for the human OS. You'll learn more stuff and become better, but they are investing in themselves more than in you. Whenever I did a training course in my corporate days, I'd be thinking about how I could stealthily apply what I learned to my own life. I used their time to reinvent myself. We can all apply what we learn wherever we happen to be. Paying attention to the world around us is more valuable than ever, because change is happening so fast that we can see it on the street long before it's ratified by research findings, appears in social commentary or populates corporate financial results.

IF WE WANT CHANGE WE HAVE TO INITIATE IT OURSELVES — NOT WAIT, NOT ASK FOR PERMISSION, JUST GO.

The good news about reinventing ourselves is that all the gatekeepers have left the building. We can learn anything we want, on any topic, drawing on the world's best thinkers, mostly for free. This has never happened before. On the one hand, people are worried their jobs and industries are disappearing; on the other, we all have the gift of choice on what we do about it. We can whinge while we watch another reality unfold, or we can draw on the potential we all have to reinvent ourselves. We can go out there and learn new things, create new value and start anything with next to nothing, other than time. Yes, the changes are mind blowing, but so are the choices on what we can do about them.

How to become ... anything

I used to be so skinny I got teased at school. My friends would say, don't open the door, it's windy out there, Steve will blow away. For a teenager any type of teasing hurts, so I was kinda scarred by it. I got a bit obsessed with losing my nickname, Pencil Neck, and I hit the gym big time. I knew absolutely nothing about weight training, except that people said lifting weights, over time, builds muscle mass and beefs up even a skinny guy. I went at least five times a week for many years. Within three months I knew I'd achieve my goal; after a year I was physically a different person. All I did was work hard in the gym for 45 minutes a day and eat healthily.

No tricks, no special food, no enhancements. All I did was change places. I changed where I invested my time after work, and it transformed me physically. But I noticed some interesting things in the process. If we continually show up at a place where a certain thing happens, the place itself teaches us what we need to learn to be successful at that thing. I got talking with other weight trainers. We shared ideas and tips. We watched each other and learned lifting techniques from each other. We discussed food and books to read. We also motivated each other to do our best. It was a really cool experience, because weight training is both personal and collaborative. No two bodies are the same shape or have the same potential. So you run your own race, and it's up to you to develop your body's potential. You get immediate feedback on how strong you are becoming, but you don't see physical progress for some time. But gym junkies also collaborate with each other. We 'spot' for each other, ensuring we push ourselves to our maximum potential. We watch our collective progress, and we all hate missing a session. Through this process, you learn what works best for you; you take some advice and ignore other bits. You try out different things — some work, some don't. You even invent your own techniques. You use what you learn to develop your own regime.

Weight training gave me the confidence to do anything in life. If you can reshape your body, then surely you can reshape your life. It's the only sport I know where you 'wear' how good you are at it. This strange fact then evolves into an interesting social situation. Once people in the gym see how well you lift weight and the shape you're in, they start coming over and asking for advice. I'd been in the gym long enough to be able to offer the best advice possible for anyone wanting to reshape their body. I'd tell them, 'You have to show up, every day'. They'd laugh and say, 'Oh, I know that, Steve, but really, what are some of the best things I can do?' I'd reiterate that showing up is the *only* thing that matters. That just being in the gym regularly enough will mean you'll learn what you need to know. And you won't want to waste the sweat on a poor diet either. I'd tell them, 'You'll only make friends with those who show up often enough, and guess what, they are the ones in the best shape. They'll respect that you show up and they'll share their ideas with you'. I'd assure them that they'll soon become hungry enough to learn the best methods and not waste their time.

Everything we need to know will be provided if we just show up — often. Frequency is more important than depth. Effort compounds in the same way investment returns do. Frequent deposits into doing something will have a greater impact than a single big block of time will. One hour a day at the gym is far more valuable than five hours on Saturday. For some reason we all try to find a way to clear up some future Saturday to do that project, when what we need to do is invest the first 10 minutes on it *today*.

I learned how to do it by doing it. I'm pretty certain that's the best way to learn anything. Sure, this book will help you with some ideas, but the ideas become your version of them once you start implementing them. You've already begun your journey to learning things that didn't make it into the classroom by reading this book. The fact that you're still reading at this point means you're the kind of person who shows up. You will have had your own weight training equivalent at some time in your life, that time you got obsessed with doing something really well. A sport, a hobby, a skill, a game, anything. It taught you because you put in a consistent effort over time. The best part of your future lies in repeating that process.

The 10-meeting method

There's another way just showing up can change your circumstances. People find it difficult to change industries for all the reasons I've already mentioned — the linear thinking, the risk the employer takes, just the simple inertia of doing what they've always done. But there is a way to hack the system, and it never fails for anyone who follows it through to the end. I call it the 10-meetings method. It goes like this.

If you want to get into a gig in a new industry, all you need to do is meet with 10 people in that industry. The hardest part is usually getting the first meeting, but you can hack that process. Most of us will have a friend or colleague who knows someone we can meet with. But if you don't know anyone in the industry, turn up at an industry event in your city and be a nice human being, and you can make a new connection. When you set up the first meeting, it is important they know *you are not looking for a job*, even though in the long run that is your goal. Instead, in the meeting setup phase, you will convey simply that you find industry X interesting, and that you'd like to catch up with them for 15 minutes to learn a bit more about it.

At this point you've done a few important things. You have connected through a warm introduction, not a cold call.

You've removed the fear that you want something they can't promise — a job. You've established that you respect their time by asking for only a short meeting. It's often a smart play to offer to shout their morning coffee at their local café. Most people will give you more than 15 minutes anyway, because you've stroked their ego a little (we've all got one) by recognising their expertise.

The meeting should be about asking smart questions. If you can't think of any, outsource the process to your favourite search engine. Ask about their career trajectory, how they got there (everyone's favourite topic), the future of the industry as they see it, maybe a book recommendation, and some carefully considered questions in response to what they say when you are together. It's a good idea to take notes, which not only helps you move up the learning curve but is a great sign of respect. At the end of the meeting, ask politely if they have a colleague in the industry who wouldn't mind sharing 10 minutes with you as well. After a friendly, non-threatening discussion and some good questions indicating you valued their opinion, only a psycho would say no. Ask for contact details so you can connect with their colleague directly and not take up any more of their time. Ensure they are okay for you to mention their name and that they said you would meet with them quickly. This next connection hinges on their social credit with their industry colleague. If they didn't have this, they wouldn't give the other person's name.

At the second meeting you repeat much of the process of the first, but now you're a little further up the learning curve. You've got information from an industry insider. You've read your notes and have even more questions, tighter and better ones. You can start to discuss rather than just ask. At this meeting you begin to develop another perspective and widen your knowledge. You've already doubled the size of your industry network. At the end of this catch-up meeting you ask for an intro to another colleague, then you repeat the process. With every meeting you become more knowledgeable about the industry, learn more about what matters and ask better questions. Meeting by meeting, you are building a network of people who know each other. You're also building your reputation as someone who is courteous, enthusiastic and willing to learn. By the time you approach the tenth meeting, you're having valuable discussions about the industry; you have practically become an insider.

Here's where it gets interesting. We know that most jobs never get advertised. Whenever a role pops up in our company, we first approach trusted colleagues to ask whether they know of any possible candidates, and these colleagues are often the same people you've been meeting with. In those discussions your name comes up. They say, 'I met with this smart girl recently who seems like she really understands the industry challenges. You should give her a call. I'll connect you'. Which might even elicit the reply, 'Oh, I've met her. Yeah, I'll call her'. Suddenly you have the inside running. Instead of being just a name on a screen or piece of paper, you're that person they know, and human nature takes over. You're invited in for a chat.

Prove it!

I've used this process often in my own life and have shared it with dozens of people and many students I taught at university, and I've never known it to fail for anyone who followed through on the 10 steps. Physical interaction always beats virtual. LinkedIn is for amateurs; this method is for players.

Often I'd be that first contact for people wanting to get to know stuff. While I was teaching marketing at uni, undergraduates would ask to meet with me. They'd say, 'I'm really keen to get into marketing. I love it. I'm really into it'. I'd say, 'Prove it!' They'd look confused for a bit and then explain to me it's their major. I'd laugh and say, 'Your degree isn't worth as much as you think, especially given everyone else you are competing with for these jobs also has one'. It becomes a bit like an algebra equation, we remove the X from both sides and see what's left. It's the stuff you have outside of your basic qualification that really matters.

Graduate 1   **Graduate 2**

Marketing degree = Marketing degree + Marketing blog

~~**Marketing degree**~~ = ~~**Marketing degree**~~ + **Marketing blog**

It's easy to see who the clear winner is. If you want to stand out, then increasingly it's about what you do that proves the passion — the informal, self-starting actions that put you ahead of others in the same space. Things that not only create a digital footprint (what people see when they google you) of your personal knowledge, but show you care more than the others who just say they do. It doesn't have to be over the top either. It's often something simple like having a well-curated YouTube channel with key videos from the industry, or writing a regular blog about the latest trends, or conducting an interview podcast series with people in the game. Through being more, you'll know more, and people will notice.

Of course you need to remember that these days your CV isn't a document you compile. It isn't even what LinkedIn says. It's what Google says. Because that's the first place anyone will look when checking you out. You need to think of Google as your 'automatic CV generator'. And the good news is you can populate it however you want. Your goal should be to make the first page that pops up on your name search a page you can control, not some social feed. Your own dotcom address, your blog, something that makes you shine, while your competitors lead off with pictures of them at parties!

It's important to set this up *before* your 10-meeting strategy gets underway. Start the process of creating something in the industry, even if it's just thoughts. What you publish today can have an enormous impact on your fortunes, if you invest effort and thought in it. And don't worry that you're not an expert; it's the process and energy that matter, and as with all things, the more you do the more you'll know and be able to offer. It doesn't matter if hardly anyone looks at it; if just one person reads it after googling you, it could make all the difference. Having your own digital footprint while working through your 10-meeting method will boost its effectiveness. You can even quote and hero the clever people you meet.

Now some of these suggestions sound confronting. But we need to push past the doubt that will sometimes enter our mind.

WHEN WE ARE BLAZING OUR OWN PATH IN LIFE AND IN BUSINESS, DOUBT IS THE KEY ENEMY. IT'S EVEN BIGGER THAN FEAR, BECAUSE DOUBT ALWAYS HAPPENS BEFORE FEAR DOES. SO WHEN WE SENSE SELF-DOUBT, WE NEED TO FIGHT IT AND FORGE AHEAD.

We must ensure we don't stop what we are doing but keep writing, keep meeting people, keep calling, keep coding, keep building, keep creating, just keep doing whatever it is we ought to be doing. Even when we are not sure of the next steps, even when we can't see clearly where we are going, we must continue to move ahead. It's a bit like walking in the fog: the path reveals itself only if we keep walking. If we stand still, we'll learn nothing.

The most valuable thing I've ever done

Of all the different things I've done in my working life, writing my blog has created the most value. It's right at the top of the list. I first started writing it 10 years ago, and it changed me and what I believed was possible for me. The reason it was so valuable is that it taught me how to slide across into new realms. The first iteration of my blog was about my personal journey, leaving the realm of the Fortune 500 and doing my first post-corporate startup. Once I started writing, the feedback I was getting from readers taught me how to write better and which posts were creating value for others. I also became curious about what best blogging practice was. The more I blogged, the better I got at it. So I began doing it daily. Knowing I had to write something every day forced me to look further afield for insights, and I started to see the world more clearly. I paid more attention to my own startup journey so I could share the lessons.

Because the blog was at the pointy end of the Web 2.0 revolution (remember, this was before the social media boom), it also taught me a lot about technology. I learned the art of the mash-up and how to hack blogging software and use the platform. I learned how to link seemingly disparate things and ideas and how to promote my work through digital forums. It taught me to think better, to propose an argument to my readers, because every blog post is a mini pitch. I made new connections with others in startup land through the blogging and startup community who were interested in the topic. Weirdly, the startup community thought my ideas were fresh, but all I was doing was weaving some classic marketing methodology through the emerging digital layer, which turned out to be something a lot of techies had never been exposed to before. It taught me just to do things and not wait to be picked, like okay Steve, you're now qualified enough to write about startups.

Remember, we are what we do, and I showed up every day. Through my blog, I invented a new career realm. It turned me from a corporate guy into a startup guy. The first post-corporate startup I did was a disaster. I lost my shorts, but the blog, sharing the failures, was a success. It gave me the confidence to keep going. My next startup did very well.

Blogging helped me understand that my life could become a series of transitions. I could take one skill and turn it into the next one. In big business they call it related diversification. I like to call it portfolio living.

The portfolio of you

Our chances of guessing how we'll be earning our income in 10 years' time are very low — close to zero, in fact. What we can assume is that it will change from today, that it will involve more than one revenue stream and that we'll need to learn a bunch of new skills to cope in that environment. We won't need to learn how to do something new, the x, y or z skill per se. We'll instead need a bunch of new methodologies and intelligences that will allow us to adapt on demand. Understanding the impact of a new technology will be significantly more important than knowing how that technology actually functions. It will pay to focus on the human impact of it. In future our incomes will depend on our ability to coordinate activities with other people, on our ability to work with various forms of artificial intelligence, on managing things collaboratively, on not being afraid of mistakes, and on running lots of little economic experiments to see what new things work. Learning in this way will allow us to build a micro-economy of revenue streams for ourselves.

The first thing anyone learns in investing is to diversify their risk, to make a range of investments so if one turns bad, they have the others; they average each other out, just as happens in an index fund. Which makes me wonder why people don't take this simple precaution in regard to their own revenue streams. It just makes sense. Having a single employer is like investing all your money in one stock on the share market and hoping it all turns out okay — not a very robust strategy.

Now let's add this thought: One boss is not a very good sample size.

I'd much rather have the market determine how good I am than a single person. Like it or not, your boss or manager has a big impact on your fortunes inside a company, so being liked is way more important than being good. They're just humans, and humans always have their favourites. There's a lot riding on your boss having your best interests at heart.

A BOSS CAN NEVER REPRESENT THE MARKET; ALL THEY'LL EVER BE IS AN OPINION. A SAMPLE SIZE OF ONE.

Robustness of sample size is something that researchers talk a lot about. In simple terms, it's the idea that we can really understand if something is true or is valued by the market only once we've tested it enough times or with enough people. I'd rather trust the market than a single person. The market is a weird and wonderfully varied place with a wide diversity of people and opinion. Some will align with us, some not. Placing our financial future in the hands of a single decision maker is less than robust, as a single disruptive event can cast us from 100 per cent to 0 per cent income.

So why restrict yourself to one boss when you can spread your risk? This is an incredible hack in the modern age, one that was nigh impossible even a decade ago. It reduces the risk of one revenue stream drying up. It gives us a better chance of finding good bosses and higher paying work. We learn to adapt more quickly and develop different skill sets. All of which make us more future proof.

You are an entrepreneur — right now

While the ideal earning scenario for any person is to have a portfolio of revenue and more than one boss, that is unlikely to happen until we become an entrepreneur. At this moment you may not see yourself as an entrepreneur, especially if you currently have a job. I've got good news for you: you'll be an entrepreneur by the end of this paragraph. It doesn't require you to do anything except change how you see the world, because you are already an entrepreneur. Yep, you're an entrepreneur right now. Even if you are reading this on public transport on the way home from cubicle land. You're an entrepreneur but you just haven't realised it yet.

We are all entrepreneurs, because we all work for ourselves. I work for Steve Sammartino Corporation. You work for [*insert your name here*] Corporation. Whether or not you have set up the formal structure, you're the CEO of your own personal corporation. We are 100 per cent in charge of our own revenue streams, brand positioning and distribution in the market. Instead of having an infrastructure and multiple customers, our mind and body is our infrastructure and our employer is (for many of us) our single customer. We are and will always be entrepreneurs. We just need to flip our thinking, and once we do everything changes. I know because when I learned this, the world changed for me.

Once we see ourselves as entrepreneurs, regardless of our circumstances, we can start to ask ourselves some interesting, potentially revealing questions:

» How are you currently treating your biggest customer?

» Would you pay yourself what you earn from your biggest customer?

» Are you creating more value than you extract from your current customer?

» Is your 'brand' indispensable and unique to your customer?

» What value proposition does your brand hold in the market, and could you find new customers immediately if the existing one (your employer) went elsewhere?

These are the questions customers ask when they cast their dollar votes on a product or service. So we should ask ourselves the same questions, given that we are that product or service. This will quickly reveal the truth and put us on a path where our values and mindset are focused externally, rather than on ourselves. We shift from an extraction viewpoint to a value creation viewpoint. What this does is shift our mindset to creating value for others, rather than wondering what's in it for us. It becomes an important part of our mental preparation for the entrepreneurial journey.

Here's something to remember: *We ought to work harder on ourselves than we do on our job.* If we want to create value in perpetuity, then we have no choice but to become self-learning algorithms. We need to adapt to and benefit the ecosystem around us more than we benefit ourselves. On the face of it, this may seem to contradict what I have just been arguing, but when we do this with our new enlightened mindset, the major beneficiaries are the people around us — our customers and our employers. We've then become something bigger and more important than ourselves. This is what entrepreneurship is really about — creating value that didn't exist before we arrived. Inventing value is the process that creates the third type of money we discussed in chapter 6 — invented money. It's creating value that lives on once we leave the building, value that multiplies the benefits to you. The essence of being an entrepreneur is to realise that it's about a choice, right now, a choice we can make today by embracing a new approach and philosophy. It doesn't require us to launch a startup or even run a project; the first thing we must do involves a simple attitudinal mind shift. This new philosophy may lead us to a point where we begin to create systems and have multiple customers. But it must start with the single entity that is us.

Venn living

In future our working lives will be based on portfolios of various income sources. You may remember the Venn diagram from grade 8 maths class. It's a useful way of displaying the possible logical relationships between different sets of information or things. It's most often represented using overlapping circles to show where two different things intersect (see figure 10.1). This is how we should view our various income sources. We should do this for two reasons: it ensures our income isn't contained in one undiversified circle, but it also informs us as to where our opportunities lie.

Figure 10.1 shows how I have used each step in my career to evolve how I earn revenue. The overlapping areas show how I leverage previous work to gain a foothold on the next step in my career. Although each step was logical, much of what I do today is worlds apart from where I started. It's all about finding the links between what you do today, and how it relates to what you

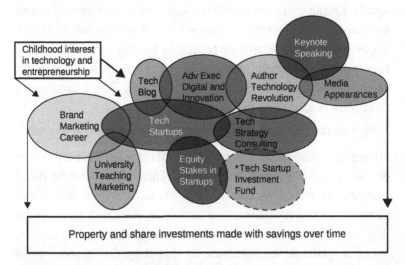

Figure 10.1: Venn diagram showing my personal income evolution and *next step

want to do next. It's not about formal qualifications, it's about doing it, selling why you belong and then learning as you go. To this day, I plot where I want to go next (see the dotted line on the diagram). Any skill and career can evolve — it just takes the effort to have a crack.

We invent new types of revenue for ourselves through identifying how what we know in one realm relates to the next. Draw up your own Venn diagram, and see how you've used this technique already. Think of the skills and opportunities in the circles you are already in. How do they relate to where you want to go? Once you see the relationship between what you already have and what you want next, you can focus on expanding or leveraging that particular skill in order to build the next circle. Over time you'll drop circles off the Venn and invent new ones.

Speed, momentum and success

While we are on the topic of grade 8 maths, there's another, totally simple equation worth remembering. This one relates to momentum. We intuitively know what it means. We hear talk about people, businesses or trends as having momentum in a very positive sense. In mechanics, momentum is the product of the mass and the velocity of an object. The Sammartino definition is a bit simpler:

Momentum = how big something is × how quickly it moves

Hence the momentum of anything will increase if either its size or the speed it moves at increases. This means that to build momentum we only need to move faster. In life, in any of our projects or money-generation activities, we don't need to be 'big' to gather momentum. A small thing moving fast uses its speed to generate momentum. At this stage, being small is an advantage. As the world is changing so rapidly, the small can change direction quickly and move more swiftly towards the future. Big things with a lot of momentum but very little speed often find it hard to change direction.

Big things, by definition, generally move slower, and big things are often facing in the wrong direction. Disruptive technology arrives at warp speed, which is why so many big companies are getting disrupted. It's not that they don't have momentum or power; it's that they move too slowly because of it. Long-time Fortune 500 companies have the laws of physics against them. As individual actors in the marketplace we ought to use this to our advantage.

So the lesson is straightforward. The most effective thing we can do to future-proof ourselves is to move quickly, because we are each small by definition (a single person). We know how slowly companies and most people move, so trying out more things more often puts us way ahead, at a time when knowing what's new matters more than ever, and it invents new money. By doing and learning things faster than others, we'll have the advantage of gaining momentum and progressing more quickly using the feedback loop.

The feedback loop

Mistakes are your friend. They are not the opposite of success, but the path towards it. They are part of the progressive realisation of success. The opposite of success is not failure but inertia, a lack of movement towards something we desire. In startups we often say it's good to fail fast and fail often, but this idea deserves some explanation beyond the rhetoric. Startups are trying to discover new business models, often using new technology. In this sense they differ from a small business, which I define as a business for which there is an existing, functional business model — like, say, a café or a local legal firm. People who start these businesses know what to do; they understand the business model and just need to execute it. A startup, on the other hand, is a discovery process. We are trying to invent something completely new, a system that can be converted into a bona fide business. So the more often we test ideas and they fail, the closer we get to finding out what works in the real marketplace. We can cross that misstep off the list and quickly move to the next idea, then the next one and the one after that. The shorter the feedback loop, the higher our likelihood of success. Every iteration moves it a step closer.

Everything we ever learn to do in life involves failure — think of important basic skills like learning to eat, walk and talk, and yet we had no fear of trying those things. It's ironic that we learned these skills before school indoctrinated us with the fear of failure. I was lucky enough to meet Australia's preeminent comedian, Wil Anderson, to record a podcast recently, and we got onto the subject of learning to be a standup comedian. If there ever was a calling that necessitated failure on the path to success, then being a standup comedian must be up there. Wil told me that once he had decided he wanted to be a comedian, he knew he had to go through a period of being bad at it. He did every gig he could, and would even drive an entire day to get a shot in front of an audience when the cost of the fuel for his car was more than he got paid. He knew it was just a matter of practice, in the real world, getting real feedback.

The cool thing is that when doing comedy you get feedback every few seconds on how well you're doing and if you are improving. So it's got the best feedback loop there is. This is what we should be aiming for with our work — the fastest feedback loop possible. This means not waiting for an annual review that might not turn out as well as we'd hoped. We need to invent feedback loops where they don't currently exist, and to ask for daily feedback on how well we are doing if it's not as obvious as it is for a comedian. The more frequent the feedback, the quicker we move up the learning curve. This is one of the reasons that digital firms can iterate so quickly and beat their industrial counterparts — all their user feedback is constantly tracked.

Whenever we connect with someone, publish to the web or do anything to enlarge our personal portfolio of skills we're sure to receive feedback. It's worth paying close attention to our own feedback loop not only to monitor how 'the market' responds to our work, but to ensure we gravitate towards those who appreciate what we do so we enter a positive spiral of growth.

CHAPTER 11
Freelancing is rad

Traditionally a limited number of roles typically seemed to fall into the freelance basket. Think freelance journalist, freelance architect, freelance actor, freelance artist, freelance web designer, freelance computer programmer, freelance bookkeeper. They were often tasks that a company or person needed only sporadically, so they'd hire the skills they needed on demand. But looking at a definition of the term can help open our mind to the true breadth of its possible application.

Freelance: Self-employed and hired to work for different companies or people on particular short-term assignments.

With such a definition, limiting 'freelance' to particular types of work seems like old-world thinking. Surely any job at all can become freelance? As the friction of employment is being removed, many people are taking the opportunity to freelance their skills. Friction of employment has been one of the major reasons we've traditionally worked at one place as employees for long periods. It was time consuming and expensive to find the right people with the right skills in the right location at the right time and at the right price. We all know this is no longer the case. We can now assess someone's personal brand reputation with a simple web search, and increasingly the tools of technology allow a separation of labour and location. For many roles in the modern economy we no longer have to be in the same place as the person hiring our skills. Silicon allows us to border hop and work anywhere we choose, to arbitrage wage disparities across countries. Reduced friction translates into freelance potential for all, no matter what we do.

A win–win solution

We can see the seeds of this movement in the startup realm perhaps more than anywhere, which is another great example of why we need to look to the fringes to see what's coming next. Roles that traditionally would literally have no place except inside the largest of companies are being hired by the week, the day, the hour — or more often by the project itself. I've been a marketing consultant for startups for half a day at a time to help them develop a brand or media strategy. Now information has been let loose, more people are not only aware of the wide array of skills out there, but they can also easily find each other.

Freelance workers have a great feedback loop. Because they have a number of customers, some simultaneously, they get wide and varied feedback on their performance. Another benefit of single-project scenarios is they can add more value more quickly. They aren't hemmed in by a company culture and methodology; they are outcome focused and don't let the system own them or eat their creativity. I believe there will soon be companies with zero employees. I don't mean a small startup either, but large, powerful Fortune 500 firms where every single 'staff member', if you can call them that, will be a freelancer.

A company of independent contractors selling their skills, project by project, will allow both the company and the people inside it to breathe. The company reduces its costs by not having to pay people in unproductive times just because they happen to be in the building. And the people don't have to look busy at slack times when they are just in the building. Those savings mean we get paid for the value we create and don't have to waste each other's time with corporate pretence in down times. Small autonomous groups form to solve a particular problem for a corporation for a time and a price. We already see this with economic platforms of the likes of Uber and the mobile app economy. Both parties will benefit from the flexibility and interdependence. Staff hierarchies disappear, with both parties making decisions based on their own economic and social rationales, rather than on what the 'boss' says. The best freelancers never ever forget that the people hiring them are not their boss, because they are their own boss and choose who they work for. We ought never be afraid of sacking a bad boss or client.

You'd be surprised at how easy it is to become a freelancer. It's worth setting up a side project to see if you can do some work, the type you do day to day for your employer, for someone else instead. You can do the work at night or on weekends. Another cool thing about it is that because your skills are discrete (say, bookkeeping) you can do this work without being in conflict with your employer, who is most likely in some other business (not bookkeeping or skill XYZ itself). You'll learn how to find a potential customer, market yourself, make a sale, keep a deadline, create some value for others and, most importantly, do it all independently. This little action can be the most incredible self-ESTEEM booster; it could even change your trajectory permanently. You might also be surprised by how much you can earn doing this.

You're worth more than you think – freelance pricing

Independent digital craftspeople are arriving thick and fast. This means all of us, by the way; we are all digital craftspeople no matter what we do, because it's the digital tools of connection provided by the web that allow us to trade our skills, no matter what they are. One of the trickiest aspects of working freelance is knowing how to price it. Getting it wrong is scary, as it can mean the difference between winning the work and seeing it go to someone else and ending up with nothing. So we tend to price our work low to be on the safe side and ensure we get the business.

There are a few things to remember here. Firstly, just because much of the first wave of internet freelancing was from low-cost labour markets, it doesn't mean 'lowest price' is the reason people are looking for freelance projecteers. All is not as it seems. One of my income sources is public speaking, in which I share my thoughts on technology strategy and the future. The first year I started doing this I was busier than expected and it started taking up too much of my time. Demand was outstripping supply, so I did what any economically minded business would do (remember, I work for Steve Sammartino Corporation) and put the price up. I figured, I'm too busy and if I put the price up demand will drop. So I raised the price by 30 per cent, expecting I'd probably get 30 per cent less business, but a strange thing happened: I got more work. The same person, with the same skills and a higher price, got busier? Doesn't make sense, right? It turns out that certain customers didn't even consider options below a certain price point. Regardless of the person doing the work, their belief is that some things should be a certain price or the quality of the work is unlikely to meet their standards.

This happens often with overseas employees such as computer coders; people have a bias that tells them that 'cheaper' (or rather, less costly) work just can't be as good. Which we know isn't true. Our smartphones work pretty well, and most of them come from China. I was told by my speaking agent that certain clients only consider speakers above a certain price, so while I became too expensive for some people, I entered a new market for others. A financial hack that many people in the services business often forget is that time is the asset we sell, and we can price it differently, and vary it quickly, based on the feedback loop. When people doing freelance service work complain to me that they are too busy, I say, 'Why don't you double your price? You'll probably only lose half your customers!'

Of course that would be the ideal situation. Half the work for the same income. It is another reason freelancing is better than wage working. An employee can't put their price up when things get too busy at work; instead they're stuck with a negotiation based on yesterday's price. Here are some hacks to remember in order to get your freelance pricing right.

My rule of thumb is you should demand at least double the rate you would earn in full-time employment doing similar work. A $20/hour in-house rate ought to be charged out at $40 an hour; if you'd earn $50 000 a year as an employee, then your freelance rate should be $100 000 per annum, and so on. If you need to charge out your work for a day, just divide your doubled annual salary by 52 to calculate the weekly rate, then divide that by five for your daily rate. If you think you have been underpaid in previous jobs, or the one you are doing as a wage earner, then you should double the rate you think you *should* have been paid. Then, in year 2, you need to double your rate again. The ultimate goal should be to charge 5-10 times what you would generate as a wage. This is because doing freelance is about the value you create, not the time it takes. So much 'wage time' is wasted 'corporitising', just being present, in meetings and waiting for the moments when value is created. Freelance work is about the value, and should be charged for accordingly. But mostly getting the price you're really worth is about confidence and branding, not time in the building.

Remember, of course, that being independent has added costs and we need to take these into account when setting our prices. This is why wages are far lower than the value employers hope to extract for them. Even in the location-agnostic digital world we still have real costs — home office materials, electricity, data, equipment and travel, for example. No one is providing us with paid annual leave and public holidays, health insurance, superannuation/401k and so on. But there's more to it than that.

We need to put ourselves in the shoes of the person or company looking to hire the skills we can provide. By assessing things from the perspective of the end customer, we can draw a much clearer picture of what we are really worth. When we do this, the *double your price* idea won't seem nearly as opportunistic. Here are a few things to remember when setting your own prices, so you can do it confidently.

» It usually costs around 50 per cent more than a person's wage to employ them. Office costs, management, administration, payroll taxes, annual leave payments, public holidays and the like add up. This is part of the calculation of prospective hirers. They always consider the substitutes and make their own calculations comparing freelancers and full-time employees, so the premium on your rate is not nearly as high as it seems.

» It is quite likely they only need your skills temporarily. Short-term resources always come at a premium; just think of the price of renting a hotel room for a night versus leasing an equivalent space for a year. So, too, for short-term labour. Convenience and short-term solutions always come at an increased price.

» Chances are the 'buyer' can't afford you all year, and while your cost per day might be much higher than it would be per day for an employee, you are most likely still a much cheaper option overall. You will be saving them money.

» Smart employers know that much of an employee's time is eaten up by 'the office paradigm' — the job takes as much time as is allowed for its completion. This is less the case for freelancers, who are usually far more effective in output per hour.

» Price is always a perception game. Our natural and automatic perception is that higher priced goods are of better quality. Pricing sends a stronger signal to potential buyers than anything else in purchasing decisions. And, contrary to what we might believe, pricing ourselves too low has as much potential to lose us work as pricing too high. Never forget that the most attractive feature of a Mercedes-Benz is the price itself.

» It's easier to find people who will pay the right rate than it is to make a living working for half of what you're actually worth. It's better to hunt a little harder to find a premium customer. They also tend to appreciate your work more than cheapskates and take the advice they are buying seriously. The respect and pride shared by both parties is what creates the 'repeat purchase'. The least loyal customer you'll find is one who buys on price. They see you as a commodity and will treat you as such. Selling yourself too cheap means you'll have to spend more time chasing new customers.

» Finally, we need to embrace the idea that price is an experiment. It is the easiest thing to change in our offer — in any business for that matter. And we can do it without notice. Over the years of catalogues, discounts and special offers in the retail world we live in, we've all been trained to expect prices to vary. Why should a freelancer be any different? It's worth remembering this:

people won't freak out if you change prices — they're used to it. So you can play with your prices. In the end it is about finding the right balance between demand and the personal supply of hours you have available.

There's one more factor to the think about: freelancers who don't price themselves right don't stay around too long. They realise the truth about pricing and often struggle before they disappear from the market. Sure, there is always a customer willing to use the 'lowest price option', but are they customers you really want? It also very often turns out that those chasing the cheapest price are the worst customers to have and the hardest to work for, because they don't respect the work you do.

FREELANCE WORK IS ONE OF THE GREATEST BRIDGES TO INVENTING MONEY; IT'S THE MISSING SEED MANY OF US CAN PLANT ON OUR PATH TO ENTREPRENEURSHIP.

Portfolio theory and the projecteers

The reason I'm so bullish on freelance work is that it's the easiest way to move up the type-of-money hierarchy. While freelance money is basically still type 1, 'earned money', it's a great way to start the transition from earned to invested and invented money, all by using the skills you already have. Moving from employee to freelancer (or *projecteer*, as I like to call it) is the start of moving from one boss and one revenue stream to multiple streams of income and a de-risked financial future.

The age of the projecteer is rapidly approaching. Many successful companies view employees as a cost centre and nothing more. Very soon employers will realise that they don't actually need employees. They'll work out that the thing they actually need is tasks completed, projects managed and leadership provided. A connected society will deliver better financial outcomes for the corporation as well. It's not just that they won't want to pay five days' labour for something that takes three days. They won't have all the added administrative costs, including providing office space, that go with a full-time workforce. Their costs will be reduced, and part of that will go to the projecteer. In some ways, this is already happening on a macro scale, with large successful companies outsourcing their manufacturing or advertising or distribution of goods. This trend will continue and we should be thankful, because it's here we use the trend as a self-conversion process.

Freelance project work can be the start of our shift to independence. It's where we learn to have more than one customer for our personal services corporation. It's where we gain confidence in our ability, build our personal or micro brands, and gain new connections and reputation for future projects.

Another thing we can start to do is employ others to take on part of the work for us — that is, we can start to arbitrage labour. *Arbitrage* is the process by which we sell something for a higher price than we bought it for in different markets. This is essentially what all employers do when they give someone a job. Becoming a freelance projecteer, we can start to organise the factors of production instead of being them, but it's a nice soft entry point where in the first instance we just sell our time. As we get more experienced at doing it, we can experiment with building a system around it, a small business, something bigger than ourselves. It's how most services businesses start; legal firms, architecture firms, accountancy practices, consultancies — they all start at some point with a single freelancer.

The rules change for freelancers. You can become a company and reduce your tax burden from the top rate to the corporate

rate. Crazy, huh? It's the same work, you're the same person, but because you have more than one customer you suddenly have the right to set up a corporate structure with major tax advantages. Lower tax rates, expenses you can claim that people can't, and certain benefits that wage earners just don't get because the system has not been set up for their benefit.

The greatest freelance hack of all time

In 2013 it emerged that an 'enterprising' software developer had outsourced his actual job to a freelancer based overseas.[19] The employee contracted his work to a consulting firm in Shenyang, China, for a fraction of the money he was being paid. Clearly this involved some serious security breaches against his employer. He opened up their network, FedExed specific security log-in details to his Chinese subcontractors and seriously gamed the system. As you would guess, once it was discovered he was fired. I often wonder if I would have promoted him and said, 'Teach us how to do this better in more areas of our firm!'

What's interesting is that there was nothing stopping this employee from proposing it to his company, or going out and competing against his current employer in the work that he was doing. He was clearly better at doing it cost effectively and was great at managing his team. It was the security breaches that upended him, not the idea, or quality of the work.

The world is an interesting place, and sometimes the best ideas are lost because we don't have the courage to formalise the informal.

CHAPTER 12
Upskilling

You've probably got a rich friend who bought an early large flat-screen TV for $20 000 or so. While it's valuable to learn about technology early, it pays to be a laggard when it comes to buying technology. As we know, TVs that were once restricted to the luxury market can now be bought for a few hundred dollars. But it turns out that while TVs don't cost much to buy, they've never been so expensive to watch. The opportunity cost of passively letting someone else steal our most valuable resource (time) is crazy high. It's higher now than ever, because until now you couldn't just go and reinvent yourself without seeking permission or paying a dollar price. That's all changed, and the people who invest in themselves now will own the future. It doesn't matter who went to a better school or has a better degree; the new game is adapting quickly by having a crack at making stuff happen. The new barrier to entry is not getting sucked into the reality TV vortex, where you outsource your reality to someone else's, living someone else's life vicariously. I know you're too smart to fall for that trick. Certainly TV can be rad, the best learning tool of all, but just make sure you're the program director.

Make the market (people) love you

When you reinvent yourself, the market — which is just people — gains a new kind of esteem for you. There's something about the person who has made an effort to upgrade themselves and *be more* that we all respect. The person who left their job to start a business or travel, or to start a new career doing something completely different, radiates an aura. People notice. Reinventing yourself draws attention. When people know you invest in yourself, you are referred to in a positive way more often. People ask your opinion, they come to you for career advice; a 'bonus network' of people gravitate towards you because you don't stand still and are always uncovering new possibilities. People want to be around you in the hope that some of that will rub off, and often it does. Like attracts like, and people who care enough to make an effort usually care enough to help others, who are inspired by this. We start to feed off each other and share ideas, because we see one another not as competitors but as collaborators.

Most people embarking on this path to reinvention are smart enough to recognise that with the changes now afoot, yesterday's revenue or employment may soon dry up. So they learn about new things, about the way their industry is changing or about the technology that is impacting it, and this type of knowledge is much in demand.

There is a hidden truth in all of this, however. When someone employs you to teach them something, they aren't really buying the knowledge you have. You know and they know that such knowledge can usually be acquired online, and free. What they are really buying is your energy and your attitude. Secretly, even subconsciously, they are hoping they will be infected with your bug of making the effort; they're thinking about what it could do for them.

Become a one percenter

It's a lot easier than you'd think to become a one percenter. My definition is a little different too. I'm not suggesting you hope to be a billionaire who doesn't pay their taxes, but rather that you become the person who knows more than 99 per cent of people in the areas of your own economic dominion. Here's how.

You can be the 1 per cent of the population in your industry who are up to date on the latest information on it. It might surprise you but most people never read anything about the technological changes, and the economic impact of them, relating to their industry. What they often do is read the news on their industry. They get their updates from what's new. Unfortunately, news is of far less value these days than it once was. Firstly, there are so many sources and so many updates it's impossible to keep up, and secondly, in an age of clickbait[20] much of it is designed to keep us in the place serving it up for as long as possible, rather than informing us of something valuable.

Fast news is like fast food. It has very little intellectual value. Slow news is what we ought to focus on. Far better to give our limited attention to information that has considered a range of interplaying factors influencing change that have been brewing over time. As Alain de Botton explains in his book *The News: A User's Manual*, 'news' isn't news; rather it's a tiny selection of things that happened today that someone decided you ought to care about. It has a severe selection bias. Chances are it has little effect on our daily lives, other than to depress us. Sure, be aware of what's happening, but our best energy is spent on curating our own information from sources we respect.

Becoming the most informed person in your field can be as simple as watching a video on YouTube once a day. Whenever I do a talk about modern technology to an industry (say, banking and finance), I conduct a little experiment. I do an

Australian Bureau of Statistics search on the number of people employed in that particular industry in our country. I search on YouTube for the most viewed video on the most important emergent technology for that industry. I then filter the search for Australia-only views. Every single time I have done this, the total views of that video have never amounted to more than 1 per cent of the total number of people employed in that industry. And this is not to say those who watched it are even in the industry. Now, I know this is a very crude measure, and, sure, they could have got this kind of update from elsewhere, but it is very telling, especially given that much of this stuff has likely happened since they graduated. This is one simple hack. Try it, and you too can become a one percenter within your industry.

Just to check myself, I've just searched the top five trending videos from 'today' on YouTube and found they have garnered 18 million views in less than 24 hours. I can promise you that not one of them can help you in your life, other than by providing some disposable entertainment. I thought I'd go a little deeper and look at the most viewed explanation videos on YouTube for some general technologies that impact all of us in our everyday lives. I randomly chose Bitcoin, Blockchain and Internet of Things, and sorted the results to the number one most viewed video. Table 12.1 shows the searches made and the number of views.

Table 12.1: YouTube search terms and views

Search term	Number of views
Bitcoin explained	2.7 million
What is the Blockchain?	385 000
Internet of Things explained	564 000

Most people don't care, or more accurately dare, to invest in themselves.

Earl Nightingale proposed another strategy for becoming a one percenter. Many years ago I implemented his advice, and it has worked for me. He said if you are prepared to put in one hour a day to study in your chosen field it will change your life and your fortunes. That's all it takes, just one hour a day. If you do this, he said, you'll reach the top of your field within three years. Within five years you'll be a national authority. Within seven years, he claimed, you can be one of the most learned people in the world at what you do. Imagine. Just three years of not watching some time-wasting TV show after dinner, and learning instead. And these days it doesn't have to be just reading. It can be videos, podcasts, interviews, meetups or any other source from which dependable information is extracted. Personally, I still think books have the greatest value, because they make us 'stay inside an idea' longer and generate more moments of reflection. It's important to remember that information is like food — not all of it is equally nutritious, so be sure to go for quality and make sure it comes highly recommended. The thing I'm most proud of in my house is my library, probably because of what it has helped me become.

If you read for an hour a day, you can take in a book a week. Most books can be read in six to eight hours (you can check the listening time on audible books). If you complete a book a week in your chosen field you'll read 50 books a year, and it'll be the best financial investment you've ever made. But even if you only read one book per month, that will still place you in the top 1 per cent of the most educated people in our society. It's highly likely to put you in the top 1 per cent of income earners in that field too. Books will teach you not only what you need to know, but the tricks and social behaviours that help you get to the top. Every book you read helps you understand how much more there is to know. If you have the tenacity to do the reading for just one hour a day, you'll end up becoming one of the most informed, capable and trusted people in your field, and trust is a proxy for money. Regular reading will transform your life.

Find human filters

Beyond books in our chosen field, it's also important we have a firm grip on the socio-political environment, a feel for the zeitgeist. In times of information abundance, having trusted human filters is more important than ever. This too is something we need. I have a few sources I rely on to give me slow news on what's happening in the world:

» *Wired* magazine for general technology — a monthly magazine

» Econtalk for economic shifts — a weekly economics podcast with Russ Roberts

» Seth Godin's blog — a daily blog on marketing and respect

» Interviews with Kevin Kelly — wherever I can find them

» The Long Now Seminars on long-term thinking — a series updated approximately monthly

» Craphound with Cory Doctorow on digital privacy and security issues — a science fiction writer and commentator with a podcast updated sporadically

» My Twitter feed — my smart and trusted local friends on things I care about

» Techmeme, a tech news website — I only read the headlines, which takes me one minute a day.

This list is less onerous than it may look. Most of it can be consumed on a daily commute or just before I go to sleep at night. Getting your trusted curators working for you will put you ahead without wasting time on the inconsequential.

The impact of technology, not how it works

It's easy to be tricked into thinking we need to know how emerging technology works in a technical or function sense. Nothing could be further from the truth, particularly in a world where a few keystrokes will connect us with someone who does understand how something works. Being future proof is not about raw intelligence either. It's about making the effort to stop and think. Sometimes it's a simple matter of making little linkages on how a new technology might impact something older that you understand very well.

Let's take the driverless car as an example. The most interesting thing about this technological revolution is not how it works, but the economic and social impact it will have. To imagine how this might play out we need only think like a human.

» *Traffic jams may disappear.* Because algorithms can reorganise traffic among cars, and they even know how to drive in the rain, people might live further away from cities.

» *Cars would be like rolling lounge rooms.* Cars might look more like lounge rooms with sleeper seats, which could further enhance satellite city or rural living. This could reduce the price disparity between inner cities and outer suburbs. It might also eat into short-haul flights, and rolling commerce and entertainment might develop a new industry.

» *Rich kids may get cars for Christmas.* Car manufacturers might start marketing cars to rich parents of 12-year-olds since a licence won't be required to use it. Counterintuitively, the car industry might sell more cars as the demographic market expands.

» *Alcohol consumption may increase.* Without the check on drink-driving we might drink more than we do today. Maybe alcoholic beverage companies will provide self-drive cars as a side business to their customers!

» *These cars don't crash.* So you might not need to buy insurance for it. You couldn't even steal one as it would just drive itself back home, because it knows where it lives. We may need to insure against people hacking it, though.

» *Supermarket shopping may be revolutionised.* We could have self-drive pick-up bays a bit like a McDonald's drive-through, which would require a smaller retailer footprint.

» *Car parks may be used differently.* Car parks empty out in the day as cars 'go out to work for their owners'; at night the car parks fill up as these self-drive cars need to be cleaned and parked to be ready for the next day.

These few simple ideas I've just brain-jammed are not about the technology. I'm just thinking about some potential implications, which is something anyone could and should do. Think through how a change might affect your industry or company, and imagine some opportunities to take advantage of it.

The no-excuse list — how to learn anything for free and change your life

First we need to make sure you're capable and smart enough. Here's the test.

'Can you read?'

Congratulations, you just passed the test.

This is the starting point for anyone who wants to learn literally anything, and do so for free. If you've got an internet connection, then you have everything you need. What follows is not a definitive list, but an illustration of how we are no more than one degree of separation from the world's knowledge. This has never happened before in human history. What an opportunity! It wouldn't just be a shame to waste it; it would be a great squandering, an insult to all those who toiled before us without such an option.

» *MOOCs (Massive Open Online Courses):* With a MOOC anyone can do any university course, mostly for free, without being accepted by the university or rich enough to pay for the fees. I'm not talking about Joe Punchclock University either, but courses from Ivy League universities — Harvard, Stanford, Yale, you name it — in all manner of subjects. The world's best universities with the world's leading authorities, free for you. And what kind of courses can you take? Well, all kinds … in the Arts and Humanities, Business, Computer Science, Science, Data Science, Life Sciences, Maths and Logic, Personal Development, Physical Sciences, Social Sciences and languages.

» *Humble YouTube:* Learn anything on any topic, from the world's thought leaders, to the gal around the corner. It's all there and easy to absorb — just sit back, watch and learn. There's no easier way.

» *Meetups:* So you've watched a few videos and want to learn more and to meet others at the cutting edge of this new thing — say, biohacking or financial technology. There's sure to be a meetup for it in your closest city, probably this week. Go there, meet the people doing it and learn from those inventing the future. You never know, they might need someone with your skills to get their new startup going. You might meet people you can plug into your company or they might plug you into theirs.

» *Online training:* You'd love to know how to write computer code or learn enough to teach your kids and get them started on something you missed. Great. That's free too. Just log on to Code Academy and start within five minutes, and you'll have written your first lines of code today. By tomorrow you'll be on your way and actually writing basic code. Or just google and learn to code online — there are so many opportunities out there it'll blow your mind. In fact, there's online training and webinars for nearly any skill you could hope to learn.

» *Thought leaders:* Some of the best thinkers in the world now share with you what they are thinking, doing and experimenting with live, every day. Follow their blogs, listen to their podcasts and get involved in the renaissance of new knowledge. The people in ancient Greece and Florence didn't have access to Socrates' or da Vinci's mind and activities, but today you do. Ray Kurzweil, Elon Musk and the leading thinkers of our time share their thoughts online free as they have them. Tune in.

» *There's an app for that:* And not just one that helps you tune in to fashion and entertainment news. There are many that can teach you how to do real stuff — like Duolingo, the incredible app that guides you from zero to hero in learning another language. You can bet there's an app to do or learn that thing you're now interested in.

» *Co-work communities:* Co-working spaces are bubbling up wherever people are. Most of them run cool events for free, where you can learn stuff live and question a local expert. These are the people who are shaping tomorrow, and these are the spaces from which tomorrow's industries will emerge. Go and introduce yourself, get involved and get some modern-day town-square action on.

ACCESS IS NO LONGER A HURDLE, SO THERE IS NO EXCUSE NOT TO LEARN.

Check out noexcuselist.com, where you can find a place to learn all the above and more: music, art, cooking, robot making, computer hacking, artificial intelligence, gardening ... anything. What a great equaliser!

Everything that matters I've ever learned, other than reading, writing and basic arithmetic, I taught myself, mostly because I chose what to learn, so the motivation bit came easy. Now we all have an *a la carte* menu for whatever we want, in whatever format suits us best. We simply can't ask for more than that, can we?

Privileged Johnny vs Hardworking Mary

You might be thinking that none of this stuff matters, because you still won't be 'qualified' in the old-world sense — you won't have *the paperwork*. But let me share this thought with you. Imagine for a moment there are two kids who went to Harvard, Privileged Johnny and Hardworking Mary.

Let's take a look at Johnny: He comes from an upper-middle-class family. He went to a private school before college. He studied hard and was accepted into Harvard. He is a good, nice, smart kid. He did all the coursework, paid his $200 000 in tuition and earned his degree.

Now let's look at Mary: She is from a working-class family. She went to public school and studied hard but didn't get into Harvard. She's a good, nice, smart kid. But Mary studied at

Harvard anyway. She did all the coursework that Johnny did through a MOOC course and didn't pay any tuition. But she only got certificates of completion. No degree for Mary.

As a prospective employer, I would choose Mary in front of Johnny any day of the week. While I'm not certain who the better candidate is, there are a lot of things I know Mary has for sure that Johnny might not have. To do what she has done, she must be smart, a self-starter, tenacious, independent and entrepreneurial, for instance. She's surely got what any business needs. Most companies today wouldn't have the fortitude to make this choice. But eventually the market will recognise Mary's qualities, and she'll start to be the choice that wise people make.

The ultimate pitch method – how to sell anything to anyone

Pitching is one of our most important skills in life. The first thing we do when we leave school and look for a job is essentially a pitch. If we were not qualified, then we wouldn't even have landed an interview. The person who gets the job isn't necessarily the most qualified, but is likely to be the best at pitching. I often joke that what goes into our mouths determines how long we live, while what comes out of our mouths determines how much we earn. It's the same in the business and startup ecosystem. It's not the startups with the best technology that get venture capital funding in Silicon Valley — it's those with the best pitch. When you hear the story of someone pitching a book to publishers 20 times before being offered a contract, it's probably because it took them 20 times to get the pitch down.

It's weird, then, that most of what we learn about public speaking is a kind of quasi-political proposal technique that has little application in the real world, let alone to selling ourselves. We are never actually taught how to sell anything. For some reason selling doesn't evoke a great deal of respect in our society. It's ironic that some of our most revered business, political and social leaders — Edison, JFK, Martin Luther King Jr and Steve Jobs, to name a few — were famous for knowing how to sell the dream. Many of the conversations we have in life are simple little pitches to others to get an agreement on something so we can move forward together. So it makes sense that we do it well. A pitch was literally the first thing you did when you were born — you screamed to your mum to hold you, love you and care for you — so I know you can do it. You probably even pitched to someone in your family as recently as today. We can all do it, but we sometimes freeze up in a business context.

To do it well *all the time*, we need to make it as human as possible. It needs to be just like a normal conversation. I pitch in the same way I'd explain something if I didn't regard it as a 'sell job'. It's simple and clean and it goes like this:

My pitch method

'You know how ...'

'Well, what we/I do ...'

'In fact, ...'

Simply complete each of these sentences. You can see it feels human and natural, and it's a super-easy format to remember. The end of each sentence then informs the listeners of our proposition:

'You know how ...' [the problem]

'Well, what we do ...' [the solution]

'In fact, ...' [insert crazy statistic, fact or reason to believe].

The closing fact should be the kicker on why this is a valid opportunity or to show progress that gets people excited. It works on pretty much anything. Here are some examples applied to brands you will be familiar with.

TESLA

You know how fuel-driven cars are a major contributor to carbon emissions and climate change. *Well, what we do* at Tesla is build all-electric cars that outperform petrol cars on speed, safety and style. *In fact*, we have over 400 charging stations across the USA so you'll never have to pay for petrol again.

IKEA

You know how stylish modern furniture can be expensive. *Well, what we do* is sell well-designed, flat-packed furniture for you to put together in the home to keep the costs way down. *In fact*, we've become the world's biggest furniture company, serving over 700 million customers just last year.

DRIVERLESS CARS

You know how more than a million people die in road crashes each year, and that 90 per cent are caused by human error. *Well*, self-drive cars solve this problem by replacing human drivers. *In fact*, self-drive cars have clocked up millions of miles without a single accident.

UBER

You know how ordering a taxi is uncertain, because they simply say they'll send the 'next available' cab. *Well, what we do* is tell you exactly how many minutes it will be before the car arrives. *In fact*, if we can't make that promise, we'd rather tell you that no cars are available. This has made us the biggest ride-sharing service in the world.

These brands could have pitched using different solutions and benefits. As the person giving the pitch, it is our job to focus on the angle we think will be most compelling to the person hearing it. We also have to remember that a good pitch isn't about nailing a decision, it's about initiating a conversation on the topic. An invitation to explore.

The Pitch → Engaged conversation on the topic

Now here's an example of how you might use it with a family member in relation to a household decision:

> *You know how* we cook at home every night and it's exhausting. *Well,* we could try out this new noodle bar that has main meals for $10. *In fact,* it could be cheaper than buying food and cooking at home, and we won't waste any or have to clean up afterwards!

So there you have it. My simple pitching method, which can be used in almost any situation. Practise it in life and watch the dramatic improvement in your results. And with all the new skills you'll have been accumulating to make you the most informed person in your area, you'll be able to convincingly sell the new you.

CHAPTER 13

Instant startup entrepreneur

Maybe you've read all this cool stuff on upskilling your knowledge bank, future-proofing or changing your career and de-risking your financial position, but deep down in your soul you still hanker for your own startup. Good. That's what I've been leading towards all along, because in my view it is the greatest thing anyone can do with their career. A business or startup has added benefits, because when something is bigger than you, you can start to contribute important things to the community, like employment for others, improved products and services, and even social outcomes. So let's get to it and start something from scratch right now. But before we do that, let's get one thing clear: *going all in is a terrible idea.*

All or nothing is terrible advice

You've heard the story about burning your boats, right? Legend has it that when in 1519 the Spanish conquistador Hernán Cortés arrived in the New World with 600 men, he ordered them to burn their ships. There was to be no turning back; they were totally committed to his perilous plan to plunder the riches of the Aztec empire. Here's the thing: Hernán was kind of like

Google or Apple today, with incredible resources at his disposal. And us? Well, we are not Hernán. We are living comfortably in a developed country. We would probably not die for startup success. We, in the modern world, should be smart enough to be able to ignore this advice.

I've personally undertaken a lot of startups — more than 10. I've also been involved with a lot of side projects. Most of them failed financially. I've had two startups in which I succeeded in selling the business. But I never burned my boats. I always had some hidden away under the bushes by the shore for a quick and painless escape. Once I even joined another army (losing the financial battle in a particular startup, I went back to earning money in a corporate role). I always had some form of investment to fall back on, some cash, shares and property — my invested money. I continued to make passive investments while I was bootstrapping my startups. And it was for this reason alone that I could keep on playing the game, building another startup and trying again. I've got friends and colleagues who went all in, lost and now they have very little to fall back on.

Sure, we all approach things in different ways, but for me startups are an infinite game that I want to keep playing, so I always keep a few boats by the shore. It's bad advice to go all in, advice often given by people with different incentives from yours, or people for whom it happened to work, who have been shaped by success or survivorship bias.[21] We know about how startup X succeeded despite the overwhelming odds against it, *because* it is so unusual. So we are urged to pursue that path to success, but it's a crap shoot not worth taking. A better approach is to invest in the many hours most people waste watching their expensive TVs. In an hour a night and a few hours over a weekend you could probably get more done than in an entire week working in a job. There's so much down time in jobs. In your world there are no meetings, no approvals needed; instead you just go and do what you need to do. With no boss in your way, you do what you think is right, as quickly as you like.

Side projects and the MVP

Side projects lead to front projects; the fringe is your friend. Many of the projects I've done on the side have led to bigger things. For example, producing my own blog taught me the art of business writing. I was writing it for more than six years before I wrote my first book, *The Great Fragmentation*. Writing had been something I did 'on the side'; later it moved to the front. I did speaking engagements in my local community for five years before I got paid for one. I bootstrapped my first dotcom business while working in a corporate role for six months to get validation, before I left work to do it full time. I even managed to collaborate at nights and weekends with a stranger from Romania to build a full-size car made of Lego that drives (just google Life Size Lego Car to see it) as a side project. This opened up many other opportunities. My startup, Sneaky Surf, a technology-driven surf company, is currently my side project running parallel with my major daily activities. Succeeding on the side is the best practice for nimble entrepreneurs.

In startup land we often talk about the MVP, or minimum viable product. It's a brilliant concept that helps us cross the chasm between employee and entrepreneur. Minimum viable product is exactly what it suggests. It's a way we can test an idea in the real market, with real people, asking them to pay for it with their own money, to validate a concept before we lay down big investments in time or money. The MVP is about getting into the real market, beyond some contrived market research situation that may not represent reality. It requires the minimum output that still solves the market's problem and is viable, which is not always easy in a world so focused on size and 'bigger is better'.

IN STARTUP LAND, SMALL IS BEAUTIFUL. SIDE PROJECTS ARE THE PERFECT WAY TO VALIDATE AND BUILD AN MVP.

So many small businesses fail just because they haven't really proved there is a market for what they are selling, making or servicing, or they haven't developed their offer sharply enough. They just go on a hunch instead of proof. The aim with an MVP is to test what we call *market fit*. Only once there is proof that the product or service we are delivering solves someone's problem do we double down.

And while we are on the subject of MVPs, side projects and getting little startups going, let's not forget the basic premise of what a business ought to do. It's this simple:

The business we are in is the problems we solve, not the products or services we sell.

Different products, services and solutions arrive to solve old problems in new and interesting ways. This is our opportunity. It's rare indeed that startups solve a currently unsolved problem. Mostly they are new, better versions of something that already exists. Cheaper, faster, more efficient, more human, nicer, prettier, sexier, better designed, better distributed ... Technology is a terrific way to make this kind of stuff happen. And never forget, if you solve someone's problem well enough, they'll be more than happy to give you their money.

Become an entrepreneur – today

We've already agreed that you're an entrepreneur no matter who you get your money from, but there are some ways to get to the next level super quickly — today, in fact. You can start as soon as you read this, if you want. The opportunities for micro-entrepreneurship are many and varied. Once you get started, the energy and excitement will take hold of you and raise you to another level.

The best kind of startup is one that requires the minimum number of people to say yes. Some require more people to say yes than others. Each additional 'yes' requirement adds another layer of complexity and reduces the probability of success. But you'll quickly find out that we generate the most momentum when we don't require anyone to say yes to do it.

So here's a list of entrepreneurial side projects you can embark on that will certainly teach you something, and maybe even change what you do for the rest of your life. For each one I'll provide a very brief summary of the *what, why, what you'll learn* and *where to start.*

RUN AN EVENT

What: An event draws together a number of people on a certain date, with a certain benefit, at a price (don't make it free; remember, we are trying to create value people will pay for). It could be as simple as a movie night for a film that isn't showing in your area. It could be a demo night for a new product that people would love to try but that is expensive, such as playing with high-level virtual reality or test-riding a driverless car. It could be lining up a minor celebrity to do a Q&A session.

Why: Events are great because they have a start, a middle and an end. Once it's over you can assess what went well and what didn't work. It's a great way to truncate the learning process, to squeeze a large number of startup lessons into a short period of time.

What you'll learn: You learn the art of organising the product, the location, how to price something, how to promote something, the importance of deadlines, that people don't always do what they say they will (at least 20 per cent won't even show up), that it's hard to sell things, that there's a lot of competition out there and that time is the ultimate asset. You'll learn that things cost more than you estimate, way more.

Where to start: Go to eventbrite.com and read up on how to run a good event, then get started. Choose a topic or idea you yourself would like to learn about, price it up, choose a date and go. Learn on the fly, fail, assume you'll lose your money but gain in life experience.

HAVE A GARAGE SALE

What: Gather up all the things you own that you don't need and put them all in your spare room or garage, price them up, set a date (weekends are best) and sell some stuff. It's a great local old-school thing to do. People understand the idea, and you've been to them before so you know what to do.

Why: This is probably the lowest-cost thing you can do to invent some money. It'll clear out your house and you'll end the day with real money. It's a great way to learn about how to promote and price things, and how to negotiate. People love negotiating on price at garage sales. That alone makes it worth the effort.

What you'll learn: First, you'll be surprised by what people will buy and that someone would pay for something you'd be happy to throw in the bin. And you'll see how important negotiation is. You'll be able to look your customers in the face and watch their body language 'live', with no digital screen to hide behind.

Where to start: Put up some signs in the local area advertising the date. Tell people some of the cool things you'll have for sale. Get creative: call it a 'Yuppy Garage Sale' or 'Rich Retiree Garage Sale' or 'Just Divorced Garage Sale' or 'Aspiring Entrepreneur Garage Sale' — people will love it. Push it out on your social media of choice and marry it up with some hashtags. Set yourself the objective of selling everything you have on display.

SET UP AN EBAY STORE

What: Set up a store on eBay to sell something you know a little bit about, preferably a product you use personally. For me it would be surfing equipment I'd buy on Alibaba.com. You need not even buy the product before you advertise it on eBay. Find a place you can get it for price X, then advertise it at a 'fixed price' or 'buy it now' of price X + 1. The plus one is your profit. Start with one simple auction then build a store.

Why: This is a simple way to gain skills in e-commerce. It will introduce you to arbitrage (buying at one price and selling at another in a different market). It's low cost and can all be done sitting at your laptop. You need never leave the house.

What you'll learn: It'll teach you that the best entrepreneurs sell then acquire. The hardest thing to do in the modern economy is to sell; things are easy to access. You'll learn the art of inventing money with zero down, something property development entrepreneurs have been doing for centuries.

Where to start: Go straight to eBay, or YouTube some lessons on setting up an eBay store or selling stuff you don't own.

START A MEETUP GROUP

What: The group should meet up regularly to discuss a topic of importance to you. It could be related to technology, business, a social issue — anything.

Why: It will teach you how to build a tribe of like-minded individuals.

What you'll learn: You'll learn how to become an impresario and social leader, and how to get a movement going. In the end, many companies — and startups for that matter — are less about what they sell, and more about what they represent. Starting a cohort of believers who get together regularly is a great MVP for this process. You'll often find the people in the room naturally want to make it bigger, to turn it into a business — it's a natural human inclination. But you'll see too that it isn't easy, especially at the start.

Where to start: Go to meetup.com. Attend a meetup or two first to see how they are run. Then choose a topic/meme there isn't a meetup group for already in your area — maybe there's one elsewhere, maybe none at all. Make your choice and go for it.

SELL YOUR ADVICE

What: Advertise your skills as a service on one of the many freelancing websites. Maybe it's a business or design skill, or maybe you can teach someone karate or guitar or how to swim.

Why: It'll force you to think of the thing you are really great at. You'll have to learn to write some tight copy, and ensure that your digital footprint backs up the service you are proposing to sell (for when people google you).

What you'll learn: It's possible that people are looking for people like you to help with their projects. You'll see money can be earned outside of a job.

Where to start: Go to upwork.com, freelancer.com or fiverr.com to do something more quirky, like recording a happy birthday rap song for someone. Go to any online services marketplace to see what's being advertised. Get among it, and be prepared to fail and try again — it just takes a little more effort.

MAKE SOMETHING AND SELL IT

What: We can all make something. Maybe you're good at woodwork or knitting? Try to sell your own creation.

Why: You'll see the pressure that goes with selling something you've already invested time and/or money into making. You're hungrier to sell it. Your pride is on the line, so you'll force yourself to sell it.

What you'll learn: You've already got something you can make that people will buy. Just dig back in your memory for everything you've ever made, and you'll find it there. You'll also find out what your time is really worth.

Where to start: Make it and sell it on Etsy, eBay, Craigslist, Facebook or Instagram. Make then sell. Go!

ARBITRAGE GOODS

What: Find something you can buy cheaply at Alibaba.com (the global site that lists manufacturers from around the world) and resell it locally for a profit.

Why: You'll get your first micro-taste of the global supply chain. You'll find that the barriers to getting things manufactured for you or making things available to you are much lower than you imagined.

What you'll learn: You'll learn how much profit retailers are really making on those goods they source from China. You'll piece together parts of the logistics supply chain and see how certain countries have advantages in different parts of the business landscape. You'll see how globalisation can be used to your own benefit and not just to the advantage of big company XYZ.

Where to start: Go to Alibaba.com and search for some goods you know a bit about, something you buy frequently or have bought, and decide what to sell. Once you've done this, set up somewhere to sell it, such as eBay.

DO COMMISSION-ONLY SALES

What: Get a job selling something on commission only. Door-to- door sales is preferable to phone sales because you get to interact directly with your potential customers. Charities are a good place to start. The job is easy to get — believe me, no one wants to do it. You can work in the evenings or on weekends. When someone knocks on my door, I always say no! But I do say to them, 'Congratulations, you're going to be rich, because few people have the skills you gain doing this'.

Why: It moves you quickly up the selling learning curve. No matter what we do in business and life, selling is a fundamental requirement for success. There's no better way to learn than this. It's hard and unforgiving.

What you'll learn: You'll learn how to sell, the hard way, face to face, with nowhere to hide. You'll learn how to cope with rejection, and that failure won't kill you — it will teach you.

Where to start: Just google commission sales or charity organisations. They'll have something for you. The interview will be easy; they might even have a party for you when you arrive! You're rare.

MAKE A SMARTPHONE APP

What: That app you reckon you've got an idea for? Stop talking and start doing.

Why: You'll see it's possible to participate in technology without knowing how to make the technology yourself. It'll remind you that organising the factors of production is key. Apps are just like any business.

What you'll learn: You'll discover that building it is much easier than selling it, that generating attention for an app is much harder than it looks. But it will build your confidence and you'll no longer fear technology.

Where to start: First draw the app pages on a piece of paper. This is your blueprint. There are sites that will help you design an app — just google. Explain what it does at the bottom of each page, then take it toan online services marketplace like upwork.com or freelancer.com.

DO A CROWDFUNDING CAMPAIGN

What: If your idea costs a little more money than those I've suggested, you might consider a crowdfunding campaign.

Why: It draws on many of the same elements but requires a rather bigger investment. You need to design a product or service, you need to market it, you need to build an audience and you need to sell the dream.

What you'll learn: You'll discover one of the hardest things to learn, which is that sometimes, unless we get it all, we get none of it. In crowdfunding, if you fail to achieve your funding goal, you'll have to return the money to your backers. You'll learn the importance of the visual and pre-selling it before it starts. Crowdfunding campaigns live and die on the power of their videos.

Where to start: Go to kickstarter.com, indiegogo.com or pozible.com. Read up on how to run an effective campaign, watch some videos on how to do it, and go. Start with something small and achievable.

* * *

If you want to go really crazy, start mashing these ideas up, integrating and cross-fertilising them. There are no rules once you're out of school.

The number and range of startup and business opportunities available to anyone today are astounding. These often involve industries for which platforms are yet to be built and whose possibilities we are only just beginning to discover. It is very early days in 3D printing, the Internet of Things, privacy as a platform, self-drive cars, drone applications, blockchain technology, crypto-currency and AI. Just imagine how many things you can simply add AI to in order to redefine that category. It's a technology that is at the bleeding edge of human capability and much of it is open source, like Watson from IBM.

In 20 years we'll look back with a kind of nostalgia on how open and ripe with startup opportunities the market was.

Going deeper

If you want to learn more about the startup, then there's one book I'd recommend above all others. *The Art of the Start 2.0* by Guy Kawasaki is the best entrepreneur's manual I've ever read.

Your personal brand

These projects have a wonderful additional benefit: they start to build your personal brand. You start to become, and be regarded as, an entrepreneur. Your brand expands into something more. Your digital footprint is more than a Facebook page or a boring LinkedIn profile. You become the person who has done this other cool stuff. You become more because you have done more.

These days your CV is what you say it is, not what your past employer or past job title says it is, but only if you choose to own your digital footprint. In fact, the most important stuff you'll do in your career these days is the crazy projects that show you 'get' we are living through a revolution and that you want to be part of that revolution. The tools are all here, and they are free; all you need to do is allocate some of your time to them each day and create our own path. The cool part about creating your footprint is that the internet doesn't care what school you went to, what your ATAR or SAT score was or what club you are a member of. It cares only about what you create — or, to put it better, co-create. The audience will do the judging, not some gatekeeper, HR person or university admissions manager.

Smart employers and investors are more interested in your side projects now than how you have earned a living in the past. In Silicon Valley they say, show me what you've built. Your side projects say so much more about you and your capabilities. And they do so because there are no barriers or permission requirements to what you can do in this arena.

SIDE PROJECTS COMBINE YOUR IDEAS, DESIRE, WORK ETHIC AND ABILITY TO CONNECT WITH OTHERS WHO SHARE YOUR TYPE OF INTEREST. IT'S ALL UP TO YOU, AND DEMOCRATISED TECHNOLOGY MEANS YOU DON'T HAVE TO BE A GENIUS.

I practise what I preach too — just google me and you'll see all the side projects I've done. I promise you it's worth the effort, and the market will reward you. We ought to be thankful for the resources gifted to us in this digital revolution. I regard my digital footprint as a financial investment. I see it as a conduit between my current and my future earning potential in all realms, and probably a better investment than any formal qualification could provide.

CHAPTER 14
DNA is DESTINY

This thing goes deep.

We all know that life is a great adventure, but the pictures our mind conjures up when we hear the word 'adventure' most often relate to holidays, travel and physical challenges. Economically, it seems, we prefer smooth sailing to turbulence. We prefer the financial side of our life to be predictable, stable and linear. The alternative seems like something for crazy people with an ill-considered appetite for risk. I'm hoping you've seen the other side of the argument, the emergent truth in the connected economy, and now understand that the riskiest play these days is now the opposite of the industrial era model. And given that all humans are natural adventurers, I know you can cope with an economic adventure too.

We are all born entrepreneurs. Entrepreneurship is inextricably linked to the human experience. To explore, to understand, to invent and to embrace risk-taking — these are what we've always done best as a species.

We know how to embrace change to create a better situation for ourselves and the people around us; it's why we've got this natural drive. Knowing we will fail, and learning to endure if not enjoy our failures along the way, can be the most satisfying part of adaptation.

I wonder if deep down in our human code there is not some hidden program for entrepreneurship, the willingness to take on something new, to carve out new paths and cross oceans. As a species we've settled in every part of the globe, and we are on the cusp of becoming an interplanetary species. It's our destiny. Our DNA gives us no choice but to continue to explore our own possibilities. No doubt it was one of the reasons you picked up this book: you knew there was more to know, a possible adventure, inside the cover. We need to listen to this call to adventure; it deserves our attention.

en·tre·pre·neur

Noun: A person who organises and manages any enterprise, esp. a business, usually with considerable initiative and risk. *Word origin:* 1875–80, from the French *entrepren* — to undertake or do something. Linked to *enterprise*.

Being an entrepreneur is about doing. It's more than plans, ideas and talk — it's about taking action. Being the person who will. Learning on the job. The most insightful ideas and poignant moments I have had in my life haven't been while thinking or writing, but while acting.

We are only 20 years into this connection revolution, so you've arrived nice and early. You can be part of the history of tomorrow by starting today. It took me a lifetime to learn the stuff I've written in this book, and I hope it provides you with some seriously valuable shortcuts for making yours better.

What to teach your kids

I'm often asked at the talks I give what we should be teaching our kids, and I'll begin by saying I'm no authority on child development, but there is certainly something we can all teach our kids that will stand them in good stead regardless of the way technology moves.

I'm talking about *systems thinking*. It's what this entire book has been about: how systems shape us, and how we should hack our own system.

At school we were taught how to do things, not how to understand why they matter and the system that shapes them. Learned tasks and tools can become outdated, obsolete, but if we learn how to understand a system, then we won't see ourselves as a helpless widget within it, but rather as an architect of possibilities.

When I asked my daughter if she'd like to grow some food, to teach her some systems thinking from the ground up, she replied that she wanted to grow a pizza. (She likes to make things hard!) So over many months we grew all the ingredients, including wheat to make dough (we cheated and bought the cheese, although we watched online videos on how to make it), so we could create a fully home-made pizza. She planted the seeds, helped me water the plants every day (wheat, tomatoes, oregano, basil, onion, chilli, capsicum) and helped weed the garden beds. I also explained the sources of the fire and electricity we needed to cook it.

The pizza literally took six months to deliver. But it totally changed how she sees the world. Now she asks about the processes behind everything, and she likes to sketch little production drawings of the things she learns and asks about. Every time we get pizza she appreciates how hard people have worked to produce it, and when we go to the supermarket she is in awe of the range of vegetables and what it must have taken to get them here all fresh and shiny. Now she wants to build a scarecrow linked to a computer to move its arms to scare the birds away from eating our seeds. I don't even know how to do it, but I'm sure I can find out!

Philosophy is greater than tactics

All of this comes down to philosophy, having an ideology we can use as a guide to living our lives. Something to turn to in times of confusion or hardship is wonderful in easing the stress of life. By truly understanding the economic process, our personal economics and the art of entrepreneurship, we develop a philosophy we can draw on for tactics during the game change. While there are many ways to do things, and unlimited things to learn, the most important skill is to develop a philosophy to understand the world and the way we can shape it to suit ourselves. In the long run, as we take action on the new ideas we encounter, our philosophy becomes part of who we are. While it's true that new ideas can sometimes create new actions, new actions always generate new types of thought. Our adult brains are far more malleable than we once thought; we now know that the ability to unlearn and relearn isn't the sole realm of adolescents — we can all start again. This news couldn't come at a better time, because retraining has become an essential life skill. In the past we had only limited opportunities to learn and gain qualifications; now we have as many chances as we choose to take. These opportunities arise when no one is looking; they happen when we are not pushed but feel compelled by our own personal mission.

The truth about wealth

For me wealth isn't about money, it's about how we spend our days. Wealth is measured in time, not dollars, but as we've discovered, money can open up time. More time in which to do more of the things we have a passion for and to give more love to our family and society. Philosopher Alan Watts is famous for his advice that that you should go out and do whatever it is you would do if money was no object. I'll add that if you do this, then money is more likely to gravitate towards you because you'll find your path to excellence. In any case, the having is in the doing. And in our weird and wonderful connected world we can make a living in many ways that were never open to us in a geographically constrained world.

Never forget that the only thing we really accumulate in life is experiences. When we think about the great times we've had in life, we rarely recall something we bought or the money we had; much more frequently it's the people we shared an experience with. The stories we gather from the things we do are where the richness of life comes from. Change, by definition, gives us more opportunity, enriching the adventure of our human story. Change is where the great stories come from, the trials and tribulations we can share now and later. I hope some of the stories in this book will help generate some exciting moments in your life, new experiences you never thought possible, experiences that will shape your own story and that you'll one day be happy to replay again and again.

Go.

Reinvention hacks for the future you!

1. **There are no rules for inventing money by starting a business.** No age limits, no education prerequisites, no location limits or wealth requirements. The only limits we face are those we set ourselves.

2. **A boss is not a good sample size.** The best approach is to have more than one—the more the better. A single revenue source increases our risk.

(Continued)

Reinvention hacks for the future you! *(Cont'd)*

3. **You are an entrepreneur—right now.** You are the CEO of your personal services corporation. No matter if you have only one customer, your employer, be sure you see the world from the perspective of providing services to customers. It will change your life.

4. **Venn is Zen.** Design your future as a series of overlapping Venn circles and see the potential revenue from each skill and each domain you play in. Invent your own 'licence to play' from related things you've already done.

5. **Momentum is key.** Speed beats size every time. Move quickly and leverage small advantages one day at a time.

6. **You're worth more than you think.** Experiment with pricing to find your true market value.

7. **Learning is free, so a lack of money is no excuse.** You can learn anything when you can be bothered to make the effort. Those who do apply themselves gain both the knowledge and the bonus of respect in the market.

8. **Relationships win.** Increase the frequency and proximity of meeting with people and industries you care about—being 'in the room' is all important.

9. **The best pitch wins.** Pitching is a core life skill; a better pitch beats the more qualified. Do the hard yards and *get it down*.

10. **Side projects can be life changing.** Always have one bubbling up to challenge yourself.

11. **Start the instant entrepreneur program today.** Don't wait for the big idea; it's behaviour and momentum that matter most.

Notes

1. Average median tenure of a Fortune 500 CEO: http://fortune.com/2015/05/06/ceo-tenure-cisco.

2. *Business Insider*, 25 August 2015.

3. 'Each Holden staffer costs taxpayers $50, 000', *The Australian*, 10 December 2013.

4. As above.

5. Deloitte, Global Mobile Consumer Survey, 2016.

6. 'Who are the top 100 most collectible living artists?', *Artnet News*, 27 October 2015.

7. 'Self-employed workers in the UK — 2014', Office for National Statistics United Kingdom, 20 August 2014.

8. 'Australia's future workforce — 2015', CEDA, 16 June 2015.

9. *The Future of Jobs*, World Economic Forum, 18 January 2016.

10. Facebook employee count as at June 30, 2019: http://newsroom.fb.com/company-info.

11. A price/earnings or P/E ratio is the price to buy a share based on its earnings per share. If a share is priced at $10 and it earns $1 per share per year, then it will have a 10 times earnings ratio. The lower the ratio, the cheaper the share is to buy; the higher the ratio, the more expensive the share. The multiple (10 X in this case) means it will take 10 years to get your initial investment back in earnings. Shares with high ratios are often priced that way based on the expectation that the earnings of this company will increase.

12. 'Trickle-down theory' argues for income and capital gains tax breaks or other financial benefits to large businesses, investors and entrepreneurs in order to stimulate growth. The argument hinges on two assumptions: all members of society benefit from growth; and growth is most likely to come from those with the resources and skills to increase productive output (www.investopedia.com/).

13. Companies at all levels sometimes employ 'vanity metrics' by presenting statistics selectively to impress investors, employees and the media, and sometimes even to fool themselves that they are succeeding.

14. Bill Gurley, venture capitalist investor (http://abovethecrowd.com/2015/01/30/ubers-new-bhag-uberpool/).

15. Compound annualised growth rates of S&P 500: www.moneychimp.com/features/market_cagr.htm.

16. Investment Returns on Property: www.yourinvestmentpropertymag.com.au/market-analysis/why-melbournes-properties-will-keep-on-rising-79693.aspx.

17. Past five years of S&P 500: www.macrotrends.net/2488/sp500-10-year-daily-chart.

18. Warren Buffett's final wealth investment plan: http://time.com/money/4169856/warren-buffett-retirement-plan.

19. 'US employee "outsourced to China"', BBC News, 16 January 2013.

20. *Clickbait* is sensationalised or provocative internet content designed primarily to attract people to invest time on a web page that they might otherwise avoid.

21. *Survivorship* or *success bias* is the logical error of focusing on the people or things that 'survived' a process, even though their success is anomalous and of low probability. In this way the media commonly perpetuate false conclusions. The winner is the focus of reporting in the startup and entrepreneurship realm, which can distort our conclusions on what does and does not work.